Preface

CW00971294

How we laughed at Jerry's fake moustache, but tragically failed to learn the lesson of Rex's betrayal.

In many respects this book, like so many aspects of life, is a compromise. Over the course of my life, free speech has been greatly amortised. Therefore, in a censorious society such as the UK, working with a publisher would, I believe, impaired the objectives of the book. These are, highlighting the plight of innocent WealthTek clients, and identifying the need for regulatory reform in the financial services sector. There are embedded obstacles of self-interest to achieving both of these objectives. The converse being this book was written independently. I am not a professional writer. It was necessary to manage writing this book alongside many other calls on my time. It was written on an iPhone, and a laptop. Often, I was tired, and tasked myself with writing before I went to sleep. It is not perfect, but I did my best, after attending to many other issues. The book represents my observations, thoughts, and feelings. Others may take an alternative view and interpret events differently. That is life. After 24 years of experience in financial services, I have found myself despondent, and disillusioned. Like many other professions, I hoped that the industry could be a force for good. Yes, the salaries are relatively attractive, but the industry always place the interest of client first. Despite my despondency, I still have the motivation to do my best for client. Of course, I am often self-critical, and wish I could be flawless, but, alas, we are all flawed in our respective ways. But, if our intentions are wholesome, we have a much better chance of succeeding, and treating them fairly. Please do be patient with my career observations, I hope as readers progress with the book, a logic will emerge.

I have read a good many books throughout my life and are acutely aware that a long preface can be irritating. So, here we are.

April 2024

Swimming with Piranhas

January 2000 may appear an odd place to begin a story of the events that occurred at WealthTek, some years after. I do not intend this book to be a career autobiography. That would be both vain, and, more pertinently, boring for readers. However, what I have endeavoured to do, is identify parts of my career, which helped me, via a process of deduction, form the conclusion that a serious fraud was possibly taking place at WealthTek. It was with great sadness that I wrote that sentence. Throughout the process, I had wished to be proven wrong. I would have gladly apologised to John Dance, if clients, the very people we are entrusted to serve in the wealth management industry, were spared an atrocious ordeal.

Back to January 2000. Older readers will no doubt recall the relief when the Y2K nonsense turned out to be just that. Toasters, and other appliances, continued to function, and, to far greater relief, aeroplanes, did not fall from the sky. I hope readers understand that this is not a mark of disrespect for the events of September 2001. January 2000 was the start of my financial services career. I had moved to York in the autumn of 1999, joining my girlfriend, who was studying at what is now York St John University, although its structure was different at that time. I had spent almost three years in Land Surveying, based in my hometown of Shrewsbury. I needed a change, and gave up my job, and joined her in York. I was earning very little money, and my parents were very indifferent about my prospects. I had performed poorly in my secondary education, but I was making up for time, by studying Politics and Economics with The Open University. I owe much to this institution. I funded my studies, as again, my parents were disinterested. In the autumn and winter period, I had a string of temporary jobs. One was with GNER, whose Head Quarters were located in York. My job was processing complaints, of which there were many. I had the distinction of processing a complaint from the late Richard Whitely, who many readers will remember fondly from Countdown. I recall a grievance about a baguette being rather sparsely populated with pawns. The worst job I had was a Retail Assistant at Sports Soccer, an earlier manifestation of Sports Direct, on the Monks Cross Retail Park. The business treated its staff, and customers, with contempt. The former suffered low pay, and poor conditions. The latter had some offset from low prices. We parted company just after Christmas 1999, after I questioned the modern-day workhouse format. I was the failed resistance. If readers are asking themselves if I have shopped at the group since, the answer is yes, many times. Perhaps my principles are not as earnest. Yet many of us complain about the lean model of Ryanair, but still use the airline. I was approaching 24, and a visit to York Jobcentre beckoned. It was while browsing, that I spotted the advertised position of Sales Support, at Ward Evans, in the nearby village of Dunnington.

I applied and was invited for an interview. Fortunately, my girlfriend had smartened up my appearance in the prior months and encouraged me to buy a respectable suit. The business incorporated General Insurance, and Financial Services operations, the Sales Support position was part of the latter. I was enthusiastic for the interview, owing to a natural interest in finance, and my Open University studies. The business was accommodated in a large, converted house. It reminded me of Noel's House Party. There was something happening everywhere. I was interviewed by Niall Gunn, the Director of Financial Services, in what was essentially a large conservatory. I was sat looking at a 5ft tank of Piranhas when Niall entered and interviewed me. For this short meeting, and successful outcome, I remain grateful. It was the start of my financial services career. I was only at the business for ten months, but it was extraordinarily fast paced, and enabled me to amass the equivalent of many years of experience.

If readers are curious about the piranhas, they were not there by way of coincidence. They were an image. A statement. Ward Evans was an aggressive business. Growth at any cost. There were few ethics. Commission was the God to be worshipped. But like many such businesses, the fast-paced growth, was as spectacular as the demise. I can still remember my first day. The paraplanner role did not really exist at that time. Sales Support was basic administration, and anything else which eased the flow of commission. It was explained to me that the business had little time for administrators. Ward Evans wanted staff to be commission earning as soon as possible. In the interim period, basic administrative tasks would be performed, while studying for the Financial Planning Certificate with the CII. My first study book was ordered on day one. I had yet to complete my degree. But the fast pace helped me. I sat the first paper in April 2000, the second in October 2000, and third in early 2001, which coincided with the completion of my degree. As noted above, this book is not a career autobiography, so I will not dwell on my time with the business too long. There are a few issues that are relevant, which I will now cover.

I was introduced to my colleague, Mike Bains. He was older, and more experienced than I. I must tread respectfully here. I read that Mike went on to commit fraud, which would have no doubt caused immense financial and mental stress to his clients. This occurred after the collapse of Ward Evans, but

I am sure readers can now start to appreciate my digressions. I must be careful, because I do not wish for my words to be taken as an insult by any unfortunate clients of Mike. This is not my intention. When I met him, Mike was friendly, articulate, and a good colleague. He helped me, and I enjoyed working with him. We were both outsiders to the area, and in each case had followed our partners. Mike was from Kent and told me many amusing cricketing stories. The true garden of England. His partner, a pleasant lady, was on a PhD programme at the University of York. Mike performed the funniest office prank I had ever seen. He had an uncanny skill for impersonating voices. The directors of Ward Evans were very unpleasant. In my opinion, they were bullies. One of the Employee Benefit Consultants, a likeable man called John Palfrey, often felt the pressures of the commission culture. Mike positioned himself in another area of the office and arranged with the receptionist to route a call to John when he would proceed to impersonate one of the notorious bullies. I could see both. It was hilarious. John was completely taken in. After a time, the whole office, including John, erupted in laughter. Prior to me leaving, Mike completed his Financial Planning Certificate, and became an Employee Benefit Consultant. I can recall him proudly receiving his company car, after hastily passing his driving test. I looked him up on social media from time to time, and I recall a picture posted on Twitter of him sitting proudly with a young girl, who I assumed to be his daughter. He looked so happy. The point here being I do not believe he was a bad person when we worked together. I was very sad when I read about his fraud and deception. Firstly, of course, for his clients. It taught me that circumstances and stresses can shift the balance of people. I will return to this perception later as this book progresses.

Day to day, my job was incredibly boring. This was not unusual for a Sales Support job at this time. I will focus on one aspect, as it has some relevance in the context of my thinking at Vertem Asset Management. Ward Evans was a technology savvy business. The company had invested in a digital client record system. Post would be scanned and assigned to the relevant client accounts. There were general, and miscellaneous files, to catch other correspondence. I largely had the unfortunate responsibility for this task. To break the boredom, I started to pay particular attention to remittance statements, sent to the business by life and pensions institutions. Ward Evans operated a ruthless commission model. This entailed writing business, taking upfront indemnified commission, which could be clawed back, if contacts did not meet certain persistency criteria. In essence, if policies written lapsed in their early years, commission could be clawed back. Ward Evans was very aggressive with life and pensions institutions, and generally gave business to those paying the highest upfront commissions. Research was then reverse engineered to justify the choice. They were not the only company engaging in these selfish practices, but they were certainly one of the most aggressive. This was pre-stakeholder pensions, so even a contract funded by modest contributions, could yield very substantial commission. Schemes could be rewritten as soon as the previous had passed its indemnity point. Then of course, pension transfers opportunities also came into play. It was like a bath with no plug. It did not matter if some commission was being clawed back, as long as the volume of new business overpowered the lapses. As unethical as the practice was, it was viable, until stakeholder pensions were introduced. These were a big win for consumers. Fairly priced personal pensions. They killed the indemnity commission model. Ward Evans appeared too drunk on greed to see the ticking time bomb. The business spent lavishly. High end cars, yachts, apartments, and opulent entertainment. I remember one occasion; I was sent over to a client in Otley. A factory. I was tasked with collecting some application forms. The car I was allocated frightened me to death. I earned around £12,000 per annum. The BMW was clearly worth multiples of my modest salary. The car park at Ward Evans was tight, but full of luxury cars. The company employed a full-time valet. I was sweating profusely on my return, trying to park a luxury car next to other luxury cars. At about this time, my partner fell pregnant, and we had a life decision to make. Stay in York, or return to Shropshire, and benefit from some family support. I wanted to stay in York, but I remember saying to her, Ward Evans will implode. The financial services arm had become a cash cow for the group. It ended with a client account shortfall on the general insurance side. The whole business was a disaster in waiting. This taught me valuable lessons. Niall Gunn pulled off a slick manoeuvre and salvaged the financial services arm. This was some achievement given his seniority in the Group. Ironically, it was him who further stoked my interest in investments. Platforms were in their early stages in those days. It was paper based. Portfolio analytics hardly existed. Funds were purchased on popularity. Diversification was inconsequential. On occasions I assisted him in trying to formulate a coherent narrative to clients. Mike Bains and I used to call Niall Supergun. He was charming, but quite combustible, so I thoughts drift to the excesses of the ambitions of Saddam Hussain. We left York. I enjoyed the city. As I write this book, it is with great pleasure that I see Shed Seven enjoying success. I saw them play at one of my girlfriend's university balls. They were excellent.

Off to Brum

Shropshire has its attractions, many of which I miss today, however, a major financial centre is not one. I secured another Sales Support position, this time at a business called Clay Rogers, after the respective partners. They were based in Water Street, Birmingham. I choose the term Brum affectionately, as I used to very much enjoy watching the programme of the same name with my daughter. Overall, Clay Rogers was a reasonable business. There was one very rogue adviser. He was very much attracted to Birmingham City FC. He was perfectly amenable, but very slack. He had a Small Self-Administered Scheme (SSAS) client based in Lincolnshire. They were a nice hardworking family. He was completely out of his depth. A SSAS requires sound pension knowledge, and good quality administration. The scheme was in a terrible state. I recall him asking me into his small office, where upon he enquired if I would understand if he burnt the file. My expression gave him the answer. He left the business shortly afterwards. He was a journeyman for a while, but now manages his own business. The FSA/FCA, along with the professional associations, have done much to improve standards across the industry. But sharks still lurk. It was another lesson. I recall that one day he slid out of the office to join Birmingham City FC on a bus top tour, after a league cup final. Tim Clay asked me where he was? It was extraordinary. He asked me to call him. I thought it is ok, he will never answer. He did answer. I had to think on my feet to cover for him when the noise was audible via the phone.

As I continued to build my investment knowledge and qualifications, a colleague recommended me to another business in the city, Webb Holton. They were based on Calthorpe Road, in attractive office. They saw an opportunity to expand their investment offering. It was an advisory offering, but a lot of DFM businesses had been caught out taking too much risk heading into the bear market. I very much enjoyed working with this business. They assembled a very good holistic team of professionals. The client focus was good, and we built a solid investment proposition. They were ambitious and took an both floors of the building, doubling their rent. While they recruited well, they did not drive the business hard enough. I found this frustrating, as we were an excellent team. Despite my frustrations, I did like the directors. It ended sadly. Ominous signs of cash strains. They bought in an experienced hand from the Portman Building Society to consult on the business. It was obvious what was coming. I was progressing nicely through my investment exams, with what is now the CISI, and had been applying for jobs with DFM businesses. I remember one Friday morning, I was talking to a colleague,

Paul Bagnell, who was a paraplanner at the time. We were laughing about an episode of Mike Bassett Football Manager, screened the night before. He received a call from The Boardroom. After a short time, he came back and said he had been made redundant. This surprised me, as being a paraplanner, he was useful to the business. There were further redundancies, as the morning progressed. I survived. This surprised me, as I was more of a niche. It was one of the saddest days of my career, seeing good colleagues lose their positions. I knew I would not survive another cut. Fortunately, while I had interviewed unsuccessfully for a position in the Birmingham office of Gerrard Investment Management, I had more success in Newcastle. I left Webb Holton at the end of 2005, with a heavy heart. I had seen another instance of a business overextend itself, although of this occasion, with good intentions. If I am honest, I still feel sad about leaving. Although at the time I was in a relationship with my now wife, I lived with my mother in Shrewsbury, which meant moving was relatively straightforward.

The Eagle Has Branded

Gerrard Investment Management was an unloved business. It had been mismanaged by Old Mutual, and then, subsequently, acquired by Barclays. It took Barclays a while to work out what they had acquired. They eventually absorbed it into the newly formed Wealth business, where the stock broking heritage was lost forever. I joined at the start of 2006, early into this process. Newcastle was a small office, situated in Cross House, a very dated office block. I moved up alone. I found a grossly overpriced, tiny flat in Jesmond, packed up my Renault Scenic, and drove up from Shrewsbury, just before New Years Eve in 2005. I remember the weather was very cold. I spent New Years Eve chatting to locals in pubs. I managed to survive and provide a plausible explanation as to why I was out alone. My now wife joined me in the summer of 2006, moving up from Birmingham. Do I regret moving to Newcastle? That is a complex question, which is better answered elsewhere. It was not a bad office to start my DFM career. I gained experience very quickly, and successfully completed my CISI Diploma, winning a national award in the process. Fortunately, the office took on a trainee, Chris Knowles. He moved up from near Rochdale, and we became good friends. This, along with being joined by my now wife, helped me settle in the city. I did not dislike my colleagues. There was the usual duplicity and office politics, but it was manageable. Ian McElroy was very likeable. A local, but very bright. He also performed very well in his industry exams and went on to establish his own business. I wish him well. I remember he took time on my first day to show around the city on foot. I appreciated the gesture.

You could say a schism emerged at the business, which created a good deal of tensions nationally. Alongside Barclays Capital, the bank was keen to build a rapidly growing Private Bank. They were not alone. The banks all wanted a Coutts. They lacked the glamour and heritage, but the American contingent in the bank, headed by Bob Diamond, had ruthless ambitions. Many investment managers within the business wanted to become private bankers and joined an aggressive intake of varying backgrounds and quality. Barclays rifled them all through a bootcamp of sorts. It was like an apartheid system. Investment managers associated with the Gerrard Investment management business were made to feel second class. What concerned me was the quality of products being recommended to clients, along with the approach taken. I can remember one ghastly phase that emanated from the leadership. Increasing client wallet share. Think about this for a moment. They maintained a belief that client assets were up on offer. It was a disgraceful approach. You should always start with what is in the best interests of the client. How can you help them achieve their objectives, and deliver good service in the process, when the focus is on their wallet share? We all make mistakes on occasions and wish that our decisions led to a better outcome. But intentions must always be honourable. I always ask myself is this in the best interest of the client? Is it fair? Would I take this action for myself, in the same context? They are basic safeguards that keep investment professionals on the correct path. In my opinion, the client was not always the first priority at Barclays Wealth. The culture at the bank was not right. In my region, colleagues from the offices in Nottingham and York left for Brewin Dolphin. I particularly missed my colleagues from Nottingham, although this is no sleight on those in York, who were also pleasant. It would be inappropriate of me to speculate on their motives, but they clearly felt their clients would be better served away from the business. The region held a monthly investment forum, and I used to enjoy exchanging ideas with colleagues. I have fond memories of discussions with Richard O' Neil. We both enjoyed critically discussing investments, markets, and much more. In our respective ways, we both felt the tide was turning against our autonomy, and not necessarily for the right reasons. Essentially, we were two investment professionals desperate to do our best for clients. They were challenging times, as the global financial crisis was in early formation, camouflaged by exuberance. Markets had momentum, but risks were being overlooked. The global financial crisis taught us all hard lessons, particularly in the context of leverage, and counterparty risk. Me included. In hindsight, I wish I had taken more assertive action in reducing risk sooner. In addition, the industry itself was changing. Consolidation was lending itself to more centralised propositions. Barclays, once they had started to understand what they had purchased in Gerrard Investment Management, were early movers. The approach Barclays were taking was not wholly unreasonable. The desire to drive consistency across a large network of offices is understandable. There has to be consistency of process, and outcomes, across the client base. If the outcomes vary excessively for clients of the same risk profile, some will inevitably believe that they have not been treated fairly. In my opinion, Barclays tried to do this too quickly, and bluntly. I was concerned that the profit motive was too influential. The service offering had become too bland, and it was impossible not to notice the increased role given to the bank's own products. A prominent example of this being structured products. The investment bank, Barclays Capital, being a prominent manufacturer of structured products, was significant. This relationship started in promising fashion. As investment managers, we could approach Barclays Capital and ask them to price up structured products to our own specifications. These were subject to modest scale, were designed in accordance with client requirements, and expressed our investment views. This could be geared index exposure, with an element of capital protection, or even bear notes, to hedge long positions. Barclays Capital would also make a reasonable market in such notes, which afforded sufficient liquidity. However, things started to change. The bank started to promote less bespoke notes and encouraged investment managers to support them nationally. They became harder to justify as best in class for clients. The word encouraged here requires some further explanation. What I mean is one had to justify why they were not used in portfolios. It was inferred that such decisions would be taken into account in the context of staff appraisals, and associated bonuses, under malleable behavioural categories. To what extent you were considered a team player. Highly subjective, coercion by stealth. I felt like clients were left with a bland model portfolio, masquerading as bespoke. At the smaller end, clients were encouraged to move into an actual model portfolio. Both were expensive. It was service shrinkflation. I formed the impression that the bank was readying to manage these bland offerings out of regional centres. This would mean Manchester. Investment managers would become glorified relationship managers. Meanwhile, the apartheid system with the private bankers was becoming more entrenched. I would add that not all the private bankers had poor intentions, but in aggregate, the culture towards clients were poor. They were heavy sellers of structured products, both manufactured by Barclays, and other banks. I also remember them selling an AIG cash bond stuffed with commercial paper. These investments were hammered when the global financial crises arrived. I felt depressed working for a business that did not appear to place the interests of clients first. Fortunately, an industry friend of mine, Mark Hutson, recommended me to Brewin Dolphin in Newcastle. He intermediated, and I was offered a position working for the charities desk. I could not accept the terms, as I had been promoted at Barclays Wealth, after performing well in my exams and role. I was made the equivalent of an Assistant Director, where as their offer recognised me as an investment manager. After some time passed, we again started to talk. They made an improved offer, working in a team headed by Charles May, who ran the Newcastle office. Before closing this chapter, I want to explain why I have covered this part of my career in the context of this book. The short answer is culture. Barclays provided a client money account for WealthTek, which had a large shortfall. Over £9m. It is hard to justify how this could happen at a bank of such scale, and sophistication. I acknowledge that the bank was, to an extent, mislead by John. But if all it took was a cut and paste forged letter, the UK financial system has a serious problem. If a bank the size of Barclays could not a recognise a series of very suspicious transactions, it is deeply troubling. As a bank, Barclays has a checkered history, during, and since, the period covered in this book. Look at the share price, the corporate governance, and the regulatory conduct. None of it makes good reading. Briefly skipping ahead, I wrote buyside research on the bank during my time working with Vertem. I found Barclays to be very frustrating. The bank has the potential to be good. If ever it fixes its culture, the shares would be very undervalued. But just as it appeared lessons had been learned, more governance, and regulatory setbacks would materialise. The WealthTek client account situation prompted me to take another look at the culture of Barclays. Take a temperature reading as it were. I spotted a job vacancy, posted on the Indeed platform, for a Wealth Manager in the city. I applied, and initially had to negotiate a frustrating AI suite of questions. It was possible to discern the pattern, and game the process. I then received a call from a lady in London, which was followed up by a Regional Manager, in Manchester. Finally, an interview was arranged with a member of the management of the Newcastle office. I will not name him, as it would be a touch unkind. We met in a restaurant. It was an appallingly managed interview, and he was not in the least professional. I had taken the temperature. Nothing had changed. In my opinion being the bank continues to have a culture issue. They will no doubt take an alternative view and are entitled to do so. The bank will need to carefully consider its role in the WealthTek client account. Did they comply with money laundering regulations? Did they uphold the required standards for a regulated business? I hope the conclusion reached are correct, and in full consideration of the clients of WealthTek. As I wrote this chapter, Barclays was on another voyage of reform. Let us hope for better times.

Watering Down the Old Blue Blood

I was not overly enthusiastic about joining Brewin Dolphin. Their heritage in the city was Wise Speke. They were big spenders on advertising, which was often very crass. I had encountered some of their investment managers at industry events and was not overly impressed. In someways, I saw the move as a compromise. I could see the direction the industry was taking, and judged Brewin Dolphin to be behind Barclays in the centralisation trend. I never felt happy working at the business but did learn a lot. What I would note, is Brewin Dolphin became a much better business in the years after I left. I used to write buyside research on the business, whilst working with Vertem. The improvement, which was significant, was no doubt a factor in their acquisition by Royal Bank of Canada.

When I joined at the start of 2009, the Newcastle office had just, with some degree of division, been fully rebranded as Brewin Dolphin. The Newcastle office is large, given the modest size of the city. The first thing that struck me, was it felt very disparate and Machiavellian. The trading floor was divided into banks of teams. Each with a notional head. My desk was led by Charles May, the office head. I could not stand him. I am sure the feeling was mutual. However, I could understand why he had been made office head, as adopting the Brewin Dolphin name was a divisive issue. I judged May to be a thick-skinned bully. Again, that is my opinion, others will differ. He was perfect for ramming through a controversial issue. He was broad shouldered and did not care what people thought of him. In this sense, he no doubt did a good job. He was very wealthy and was approaching the end of his career. Other heads of teams also know this, and I watched their political games with great interest. Ironically, none of them succeeded, but I had left by this time. It often felt to me that the office was merely a collection of teams sharing rent, rather than a close quartered community. I imagine that this changed for the better, in the years following my departure. The standard, and attitude, of the investment managers varied greatly. I would say the great majority were, in their own way, trying to do their best for clients. Some were very intelligent, and others outright incompetent. It is likely the balance improved in time. The lesser quality managers were mainly the old guard. Like May himself. Some did not understand a capital structure, and how businesses were valued. I remember one informal breakout meeting where an older investment manager appeared to struggle to distinguish between credit ratings and bra sizes. Another said he was selling a corporate bond fund because it held a lot of bank debt but was seemingly happy to hold bank equity. Their asset class knowledge was also poor. The younger generation were an improvement in these respects. May would occasionally try to justify his somewhat ailing position as an authorised investment manager, in addition to being office head, by random and unfathomable trades. I used to call these bidi-bidi-bum trades. It seemed like he had concocted an ill-informed idea and decided to execute it. They were challenging economic times, as the UK, and many other economies, were struggling to shake off the effects of the global financial crisis. But shares were largely reflecting this in their valuations. One day, the bidi-bidi-bum trade was the sale of Scott Wilson shares, on an incredibly depressed valuation. I knew the business, or at least part of it, from my earlier career in land surveying. The company I worked for in Shrewsbury used to subcontract work from their railway consultancy. I did not want to sell the shares and hoped that May would forget about his idea. Sadly, he did not, he got nasty, as he had previously prowled the trading floor, bidi-bidi-bum, gangling his key in his pockets, saying we are getting out of Scott Wilson. Hoping for engagement from the other teams on the floor, he was only met with polite indifference. In these days, Brewin Dolphins had an investment bank. There were Chinese walls, but as was often the case, they were a touch porous. The analysts and traders in Newcastle were well regarded. They were mid and small cap specialists, with some reasonably good brokerages. Where there was a relationship, trades were offered to the investment bank. Whilst this may appear incestuous, I believe they were generally fair. I called through to the dealers and offered the Scott Wilson trade. He called me back shortly, and asked if I still wanted to sell? I said no but was under orders. He replied by saying you do realise I have an institution on the other line straining to snap them up. Sullenly, I noted that I could well imagine. The shares were taken out some time after at multiples of the price of that trade. I recall another bidi-bidi-bum trade involving the sale of Aviva shares, on a giveaway valuation. In my mind, you need to have an opinion on the value of a security before a buy and sell decision is made. Although, being a large cap, the trades were executed via the electronic book. I do not want to be malicious towards May. He had a good client base, and no doubt performed some difficult tasks for the Group, overseeing the adoption of the Brewin Dolphin name. I certainly never wished him any unpleasantness. Life is about opinions, and I imagine he would be unflattering towards me. I hope he was enjoyed his retirement. People can often be different in a personal setting. Perhaps, we never really truly know our colleagues. We were a small team, May, Nicholas Wilson, Neil Dickinson, and myself. Nicholas Wilson, known as Nicko, was being groomed, respectively I might add, to take on the May client base. Neil was a competent and pleasant administrator. May was often away on office duties, shooting grouse, or tending to his estate. I liked Neil and Nicko. Some years after leaving, I was greatly saddened to learn that Nicko's life had ended tragically. In my opinion, he was a sound investment professional, with a good ethic. I do not know the specifics, and I would be mortified to offend any persons. But on the assumption that mental health was a factor, I greatly sympathise. Our industry has not historically, and does not presently, do enough to address these problems. Stresses builds, and it is hard to find an outlet. It sometimes seems an unforgiving industry. I do not write these words sanctimoniously, nor do I wish to draw insensitive parallels with my former colleague. However, as this book progresses, I hope readers will understand my sentiments. We got on well, and it felt that we liked each other as colleagues. Neil included. Should readers feel that I have digressed too far, please be assured. The neighbouring team on the desk included John Dance.

Again, I ask for the understanding of readers, particularly those clients of WealthTek. Firstly, at the time of writing, John had not been charged, but was under investigation for fraud and possible money laundering. It is necessary to respect that status. Secondly, nothing I write is intended to offend, or cause distress to, the clients of WealthTek, who I know have suffered greatly, both mentally and financially. I have merely written what I felt and observed. John had a varying career. He had prior experience working in market making in London, but returned to the north east following a family tragedy. I hope I have not misrepresented this. He had worked in the back office at Brewin Dolphin, in Newcastle, and had gained an opportunity to move into the front office, assisting a Divisional Director on the same desk as I. The director he worked for was quite an enigma. Likeable, charming, a little mischievous, and also greedy. I used to regard him as a bit of an intellectual parasite. He was by no means unintelligent. He was quite cunning in assessing who had knowledge and set about harvesting it quite unashamedly for his own benefit. This could be from colleagues in investment management, the investment banking analysts, or even third-party fund managers. He was very wealthy, and spent more time managing his own portfolio, than his clients. This was a secondary consideration for him. Indeed, it was concern over his conduct, and lack of ethics, which played a notable role in John and I becoming friendly, and ultimately leaving to establish Vertem Asset Management. I return to this point. John himself was likeable and popular. He had a good work ethic, and I can honestly write, unless I was gravely misled, did not have appear to harbour any sinister intentions towards clients. He was also dating Jess at the time, who became his wife. She worked in the back office at Brewin Dolphin Newcastle, and was much to his junior. That to a large extent is immaterial. John had some unfortunate setbacks in his life, as many of us have, but appeared intent on moving forward. After the WealthTek scandal broke, understandably there was much anger directed towards John. This is hardly surprising, notwithstanding the status I acknowledged above. Vinay Bedi, a senior Divisional Director at Brewin Dolphin Newcastle at this time, working on the eminent charities desk, and possible suitors to replace May, subsequently, some years later, joined us at Vertem Asset Management, and unfortunately had clients impacted by events. I came into contact with Vinay and two members of the Malloch Melville team after leaving, united in our interests to assist stranded clients. Vinay was good friends with a man called John Duns, who directed the marketing at Brewin Dolphin Newcastle, with a particular focus on the rebranding. He also had some involvement at Vertem Asset Management, as an outside consultant. He has worked the Newcastle circuit as a business development specialist for many years. Personally, I found it difficult to appreciate his qualities. He liked spending money, but it was not easy to see any tangible benefits. My colleagues at Gerrard/Barclays Wealth made the very same observations. At Brewin Dolphin, he, unless I was gravely mistaken, appeared to get away with outsourcing his own job, and celebrating the results. He also worked with two assistants. Some of the advertising was snappy, but it appeared to emanate from outside agencies, whom he had commissioned to do his own job. I am sure he has a different opinion, and respect his right to do so, but I base my words on observations. I remember one email received from Vinay, post the special administration of WealthTek, which stated that John Duns said he could never work out how a useless administrator at Brewin, could go on to achieve so much. There are a few points to note here. First, he was happy to accept money from John as a consultant to Vertem Asset Management. Second, his comments are a classic exhibit of a person attempting to be wise after the event. There are many of these in the WealthTek example. Now, I will return to the point of John. He was not useless. Far from it. I actually rate him as very intelligent. He has a sharp mathematical brain, with the ability to spot an opportunity. We can debate how this intelligence was applied, as this book progresses, in the context of how the situation stood at the time of writing. Once again, these are observations. The are not intended to cause offence. My intentions being to provide readers with an assessment of the situation, as I saw, and felt it emotionally. Having digressed a little, I will now focus on how John and I became friendly, which led to the formation of Vertem Asset Management. It is my hope that readers see logic in my digressions, as this book develops.

John was working towards becoming an investment manager, and assisting a Divisional Director, who in addition to my observations above, was notorious lazy. John was officially working under supervision, meaning he was not authorised to place discretionary trades, without some oversight. I recall that he passed this point, before leaving to establish Vertem Asset Management. He generally worked hard to help deliver the best services he could, despite his Divisional Director being at time, indifferent. In the meantime, I was helping to manage the clients of Charles May and Nicko Wilson. I was able to work without supervision, but as part of a team, would consult with my peers. In addition, in addition to managing standard private client portfolios, our team would receive referrals from the investment bank. They would be Directors and senior manager of brokerage clients. These clients were often very different in their requirements. They did not want standard, balanced risk, private client portfolio. They wanted ideas. They wanted to make money promptly. With the market still recovering from the global financial crisis, there were fertile areas for trading ideas, if the client had the correct appetite for risk. But here, there was an anomaly. These more specialist clients were categorised in the same way as the rest of the client book but had to be managed very differently. They wanted ideas where there was a catalyst for a substantial gain. Preaching the mantra of investing for long-term steady returns, in a balanced multi-asset class portfolio, was not going to be enthusiastically received. To retain these clients, from whom we generated significant fees and commissions, we had to compete with well known, usually London based, private banks and stockbrokers. I raised this anomaly with Charles and Nicko, and they acknowledged it, but underlined their importance, and asked me to service them as well as I could. I do not suggest that they were wrong. Sometimes in finance these challenges appear, and pragmatism is required. One of the most demanding was a wealthy individual who also transacted business with Lloyds of London. He wanted to grow his portfolio quickly, so he could use it to write more business with Lloyds. With the global economy still in a precarious state, there were plenty of companies in a binary scenario. They risked bankruptcy, and often needed to undertake balance sheet strengthening. In many cases, particularly in the more cyclical areas of the market, the shares could become worthless, or violently re-rate. Banking, real estate, retail, and discretionary consumption were rich hunting grounds for red blooded investors. I searched out companies in distress, which could be saved via recapitalisation, or takeover. I was often on the phone to the client discussing scenarios, and the dealer in London, almost simultaneously. I was keeping the more demanding clients of Charles and Nicko happy and helping to make them a good deal of money. John would listen in to my conversations, and was interesting in my company knowledge, and ability to switch between more conventional private client work, and stock picking with very high net worth investors. We started to talk regularly, and discovered we shared many interests within the industry. We were also frustrated and felt constrained by the culture at Brewin Dolphin Newcastle. In someways we both stood out as investment managers, as neither of us were from a monied background. We concluded that we were there to water down the blue blood, taking inspiration from The Only Fools and Horses episode, A Royal Flush. Fans of this great comedy will know what I mean, and why I choose the name of this chapter. John in many ways was trapped, and sandwiched, by a lazy and greedy Divisional Director, and a disinterested administrator. The administrator of his team was more interested in gambling, and fantasy football. His main focus was on winning the office fantasy football league. It is no exaggeration to write that he was a full-time fantasy football manager, and part-time administrator. He also used to disappear to the bookmakers at lunch and would furiously slam down his mouse if he had lost his share of the monthly mortgage. We evolved our frustrations into satirical expressions. His Divisional Director was a notorious skiver. He found endless ways to sneak from the office. Some of the excuses were extraordinary. I remember one being that he had stepped into a puddle after a long lunch, and his socks were too wet to stay in the office for the remainder of the afternoon. He developed an interest in model aeroplanes and spent a lot of money acquiring one. He managed to fly it into his own car, when stopping on a family drive. He did considerable damage. The sourcing of parts, and repairs, was undertaken in company time, with mileage covered under the cover of unsolicited client meetings. He would also tell his wife to retain the receipts for her social lunches and claim petty cash for them under the guise of faux client meetings. Such greed from a wealthy man set a terrible example. I suggested to John that he mock up a cricket style run attribution picture, with runs replaced with extraordinary skives. He did it brilliantly. It was hilarious. I also got into my mind that we could replace the word of the day from the children's programme Pinky-Dinky-Doo, with a skive of the day. John periodically kept running the Pinky-Dinky-Doo song. His Divisional Director was perplexed and did not know what we were inferring. It was our way of coping with sloth, greed, and poor culture. There were some aspects of his conduct which we both found very distasteful. Referring readers back to my earlier comments about this individual being an intellectual parasite, he would harvest investment ideas, be they buys, or sells, and action them in his own portfolios before those of his clients. We could see the contract notes at the communal printer. I cannot suggest that this cost his clients material sums. But it represented terrible professional conduct. We both queried this practice with other Directors in the office, but nothing was done to confront the issue. As long as he was generating his target revenue, they did not care. John and I were both despondent. John appeared to me as being very keen to treat clients fairly, which I respected. I would also remind readers that I was not aware that the conduct of John's Divisional Director was typical of his peers, even if they decided to look the other way. John worked hard for him and got a pittance in bonus. Crumbs off his plate. The same thing happened to me. Our directors appeared to adopt the attitude that we would not miss money we never had. I remember John's Divisional Director making an enormous SIPP contribution. To the value of a modest family home at the time, despite all the slacking he had banked throughout the year. I faced a similar outcome. They were so greedy that they did not imagine that an extra few thousand on our bonus made the difference between taking our families on holiday, or not. We were not asking for tens of thousands. Merely some recognition for the value we had added to their client bank. I can remember talking to one of the high-net-worth investors covered above. He said to me, you must enjoy all this trading we do for the commission it generates. I politely said on the issue of commission revenue, you are talking to the wrong person.

Despite being a junior investment manager, John's prior experience placed him ahead of his peers at this level. He was clearly entrepreneurial, far more than I. With only scraps to feed off from his Divisional Director, he looked elsewhere, and carved out some interesting niches. He used his dealing knowledge to become a specialist in orchestrating Venture Capital Trust (VCT) buybacks. The shares of VCT's often trade at a large discount in the secondary market. This can be frustrating for investors looking to sell for unforeseen reasons. John would collect client orders, which typically came via Independent Financial Advisers (IFAs) and orchestrated a mutually beneficial buyback. It was net asset value (NAV) accretive for the trust, and the investor traded at a narrower discount. During the course of these activities, he developed good contracts in both the market making, and IFA, communities. Both would turn out to be very influential in the formation of what became Vertem Asset Management.

I believe his initial intentions were to develop his own client bank. This is not easy to do from scratch, but he was making headway. It is also worth noting that at this time, Brewin Dolphin did not really have a coordinated strategy towards the IFA market. There were early signs of it, but it was embryonic. The old guard did not understand the IFA market and treated it with contempt. Something to scoff at, and merely a source of assets under management. They, like their peers, had only just started to work out that investment management, or in the minds of some of the dinosaurs, stockbroking, should be structured as part of holistic wealth management, and financial planning. They had started to employ in-house financial planners but had not fully thought through the strategy. Although, part of their thinking was correct, they had not considered how this appeared to IFAs, who had referred clients to the business. Naturally, some were concerned that the in-house man with a plan would start offering a no-obligations chat, as a bolt-on to their meeting with the investment manager. This did actually happen. As I have acknowledged above, Brewin Dolphin made significant process in these areas since we left the business. Meanwhile, John was approaching the IFA community with more savvy and respect. However, instead of praising John, and supporting him, a combination of greed, and jealousy, aroused the interest of senior members of this office. This was led by John Duns, who was keen, along with some other Divisional Directors, to take the credit for John's initiative and work. John was understandably annoyed, and at this point, it occurred to him that he would only ever be a serf in this business. He felt he deserved more, which was not unreasonable. The research at Brewin Dolphin, be it economic, direct equity, or collective investments, was very average. The buy list at times felt like a retrospective buy list. Full of should have been there investments, not should be there. These frustrations were fertile intellectual ground for the establishment of an independent asset management boutique.

As I hinted at earlier, the global financial crisis, and the years that followed, catalysed a wave of centralisation in the industry. Richard O' Neil and I satirically called this Burger King Investment Management in our Barclays Wealth days. But in more serious terms, investment professionals were being led to make a choice. Work at a larger business, cede some autonomy, and follow research and direction cascaded down from head office, or take the boutique route, where you can stay closer to the idea generation process. There was no right or wrong answer to this conundrum. It really came down to what motivates you as an individual. Again, as noted above, I felt my move to Brewin Dolphin afforded me extra time to make this decision. However, this window was narrowed by an unexpected event. Brewin Dolphin had been shaken down by the regulator for shortcomings in their know your client process. It was not that they were doing anything outrageously wrong, it was more an issue with documentation. I remember Tim Clay, of Clay Rogers, once saying if it is not written down, it did not happen. This would be a good way of describing the issue. It would be unfair to write that there were widespread examples of investment managers not knowing their clients. It was more accurate to note that there was insufficient written evidence that they did. There were shortfalls between what was in the head of an investment manager, and what was written down. It created serious panic at the time. But in the long-term, it was probably the shock the business needed. It was clear the business had outgrown its current Board of Directors. There was a need to professionalise, which after a few setbacks, was largely achieved. In the background, John and I would have clandestine chats about how we could do so much better. We felt the discretionary portfolios were becoming overpriced closet model portfolios. It has taken them many years, but under the new Consumer Duty regime, the FCA has woken up to this poor outcome for clients. It has become particularly poignant, as the price of model portfolio services continue to fall and will remain very competitive under Consumer Duty. It is more difficult for investment managers to justify higher margin bespoke portfolios. When writing buy-side research on Brewin Dolphin at Vertem Asset Management, I could see that this became a real challenge, as it did to the peer group. Brewin Dolphin developed a very good model portfolio service, which became the main source of growth in assets under management. Growth in the discretionary book was lacklustre. This put pressure on margins. The lower margin book was growing at the expense of the higher. John and I felt we could deliver genuine bespoke, at a more competitive price. It seemed to me that whilst the large national players had vast economies of scale in the back office, they suffered from diseconomies of scale in the front office. What I mean here is that owing to the large sums of money they manage; liquidity draws them to larger funds and stocks. We wanted to try to find smaller and dynamic funds, and businesses. Not chasing small for the sake of it, but we liked the idea of finding ideas that would be on the radar of the national players tomorrow, today. The challenge of course being, doing it without a well-resourced back office. In addition, there was the not inconsiderable issue of financing it. However, John, to his credit, is a creative thinker. Again, please do not take offence at this observation, as this book still has much ground to cover. John loosely discussed his ideas with the IFAs with whom he had built relationships. A few liked the idea of an independent asset management boutique. Furthermore, he had a good relationship with a market maker called Chris Lloyd. Chris was friends with a venture capitalist/angel investor, Harry Wilson. Wilson was experienced in the natural resources sector and held a number of impressive senior positions. He was also enjoyed success in property, and numerous other investments. A wealthy and clever individual. I met him on occasions but cannot claim to have known him well. John managed to trigger the interest of Chris, who eventually facilitated a meeting between John and Harry. I did not participate in any meeting, but to John's credit, he must have performed well. He must have sold his business plan well. One challenge remained. John needed to raise capital, otherwise the other investors would walk away. He seemed to do this gradually, by exploiting pricing anomalies on gambling sites. Making regular incremental gains. This was no mean feat. I return to my earlier point. Anyone who suggests that John is not intelligent, and afraid to pursue an opportunity, is very mistaken. I would ask him most days discreetly how it was going, and he seemed calm, and in control. I had not fully committed at this stage, but the idea appealed to me. John was also searching for infrastructure options. Essentially, working under the umbrella of a larger organisation. This was happening in early 2010. He looked at several options and settled upon Raymond James. He worked tirelessly, was determined, and made it happen. Considering he was working with little resources; this was an impressive achievement. He had developed a business plan, grown his own funding, attracted financial backers, and found a partner organisation to work with, Raymond James. Because of his relatively junior role at Brewin Dolphin, he had a short notice period. At the end of the prior calendar year, Brewin Dolphin tied their more senior staff to longer notice periods. It was a kind of shotgun deal. I recall a one-off payment of £2,000, to agree for my notice period being extended from 3 months to 6 months. Rather like an OK Continue option that we are regularly confronted with in our lives, via numerous contracts. John pressed ahead with his resignation and rented a small office in Collingwood Buildings. I was surprised that Raymond James was willing to let John establish a branch, given that he had only recent gained permission to place discretionary trades at Brewin Dolphin. Whilst it was clear that John's ability was beyond the level of his role at Brewin Dolphin, this was not straightforward to prove in documented form. It was an enormous gamble, but at the same time, a potentially exciting opportunity. When John resigned, certain members of the office thought it was a joke. They thought John was leaving to set up a VCT shop. In this sense, they underestimated his determination. I write this in the context of what I saw, and felt, at that this point in time. I missed John's leaving drinks, during his last day in the office, he smiled at me and said I hope to see you soon. It was not easy to facilitate the move, as I could not afford to drop any salary, given my commitments. Neither did I have the capital to invest in his business. He even proposed a bonus to make it easier for me to join. I know this was difficult for him, but I appreciated his determination to make it happen. I was convinced that the John I was dealing with at this time, had the best of intentions. He was desperate, in respectful terms, to break free of a structure that was holding him back and go on and achieve something. If I were to join him, it would be as a co-founder, in the sense of intellectual capital. He needed someone to generate research and ideas for the business. A boutique asset management business, providing specialist, bespoke, outsourcing solutions for IFAs. A short time after he had left, I visited John over at Collingwood Buildings to see how he was getting along. He seemed very happy. Operating on a tight budget, he was doing his best, and had enlisted some young help. Students who were looking for some experience in areas such as creative writing for the website. The business was to be called Vertus Asset Management. Bear with me on the name. Towards the end of my pre-resignation days at Brewin Dolphin, I had started work as an Associate Lecturer at Newcastle Business School, part of Northumbria University. It started as four hours a week during semester time. For this, I have to thank, sadly, posthumously, Nicko Wilson. He went out of his way to allow me to do this and knew that I was studying for an MSc Finance and enjoyed the academic side. It occurred to me that if I joined, we may be able to recruit some bright students in the future. We were both agreed that the way forward was to recruit younger staff, and mould them into the way the business would operate, rather than experienced professionals, who would be rigid in their work patterns. I would again stress this was within a client first focus, with which John was most enthusiastic. As I was writing these words, clients of WealthTek had started to view their uploaded statements, so I am most sensitive of the circumstances. Please do bear with me as the book develops. I reached a point where a decision had to be made.

I was at home one morning, and something happened which made me think, a change was required. I had been irritated and upset. I felt a change was needed. I had not even drafted a resignation letter. I travelled to the Brewin Dolphin office on The Metro, as I had run early that morning. I had been enlisted for some mandatory training, as part of the regulatory shakedown noted above. It sounded so dull and uninspiring. Role plays and so on. Nicko Wilson said to me it is time for your training. It was as if my soul took over and answered, as I plan to resign soon, there appears little point. He was understandably confused and asked me if what he was heard was correct. As I had already said it, I could only reply in the affirmative. He disappeared, and shortly afterwards I received an email from the HR lady, stating that it was their understanding that I had verbally resigned, and asked me to confirm this in writing, which I did. The initial reaction was for me to serve out my 6 months in the office. I was asked why I wanted to leave, and where I intended to move. I cited the ethical concerns about the trades being placed by John's former Divisional Director. My stance being client trades should always be executed before our own. I reminded them that these concerns had been raised with other Divisional Directors and dismissed. Their attitude then started to become more hostile, especially as I stated I intended to join John's new venture, Vertus Asset Management. I then received a call to go to the HR office. When I entered the room, May was in their too. This triggered an interesting face off. He said, do you think it is time you went home? I said, why ask a question to which you already know the answer? This was the equivalent of me saying you will not bully me. He asserted that I was to wait in this office, while my belongings were returned to me, whereupon I would be escorted out of the building. I rejected this notion, stating I am not a thief, and had no objections to the company observing me collecting my belongings. I further asserted that if I were denied this dignity, I would request the assistance of Northumbria Police. I left and collected my belongings in a respectable manner. Upon being escorted out of the building, I was humbled that a good few colleagues came to say goodbye. I was very humbled by their kindness. This included Nicko, a very likeable Japanese colleague called Ken, and quite ironically, John's former Divisional Director. I have often reflected on this occasion. I do not believe the Director was inherently bad, he was just greedy and selfish, almost without knowing it. As for May. We never liked each other. But as bad as some of his trades were, I do not believe he ever set out to disadvantage anyone. If we are honest, as investment managers, not all of our trades work out well. As for his brags that he was in the pub when someone else was sitting his stockbroking exams for him, well, I never knew if this was authentic. John and I debated it many times. In reality, we were from different worlds. I remember shortly after joining, I took a holiday to Ayrshire in a caravan. He happened to mention his wife's family owned a castle nearby. Perhaps it was the Royal Flush after all. I called John to say it was all done. He was surprised, but happy I hoped. My wife was also surprised and quite anxious. The next day I received a very hostile letter from the Head Office, containing a catalogue of threats. I really do not enjoy being bullied and threatened. I replied by encouraging them to attend to their compliance shortcomings, and expressed that neither John, nor I, had ambitions to poach their clients. However, whatever decisions clients make, will be of their own choosing. This was true, as the relationships that John had developed were with IFAs that had utilised his VCT buyback service but did not want to use Brewin Dolphin as an investment manager. I received further a further intimidatory communication summing me to the Head Office in London. It was ordered by a rather uncouth Geordie, who had previously been promoted from the Newcastle office. I replied by suggesting that we invite a representative from the regulator, then the FSA, to pass opinion on the contentious trades discussed above. She soon dropped out of the dialogue. Next up, I was to expect a call from one of the Non-Executive Directors of the Group. When the call came it was largely a non-event. He tried to say that these things are hard to identify. That is absolute nonsense, as it merely requires checking the times of trades. I went to the point quickly and suggested that rather than waste resources trying to intimidate myself, they would be better served making sure clients are treated fairly. I conceded that it was difficult to quantify any disadvantage to clients financially, but it was poor practice, and morally unacceptable for an investment manager to place personal trades ahead of clients. This was in addition to various regulatory breaches. There is always a tension between the financial aspirations of businesses, investment professionals, and their clients. But if you stop and think about if your actions are fair to the client, this serves as a useful guide. Essentially, a client has given you their trust, there is little worse than abusing it. After our conversation, I received a further letter confirming my garden leave for 6 months, to run until mid-December 2010. I have often reflected whether I took the right decision in leaving, particularly in the context of developments at WealthTek. As noted earlier in the book, Brewin Dolphin certainly became a better business. If I could have seen more humility from the business regarding my concerns, I believe I would have stayed. But it was clearly not meant to be, and a new challenge awaited me.

Investment Manumission

John and I thought of the move as escaping from The Death Star and throwing of the shackles of investment serfdom. The former became a reference to the Brewin Dolphin office in Newcastle. This was a disservice, but there was humour in the reference. I viewed my time working with Vertem Asset Management, initially Vertus Asset Management, as involving three phases. These being Vertem Raymond James, Vertem Sapia and Vertem WealthTek. This will become clearer as the book develops. I should also add that I did not own any of the business, and was engaged as a self-employed consultant, via a separate vehicle, Collingwood Wealth LLP. This is also very relevant. John was also a member of this LLP and controlled it financially. Our tax returns were overseen, and or completed, by Deborah Graham of Ryecroft Glenton. At outset, the company had no revenue. Therefore, the idea was for us both to be remunerated as self-employed consultants to the business, until such time as the company had reached a scale, where it was able to cover its costs. At which point, I would become a PAYE employee. The latter was the far better option for me, as being self- employed held no advantages. Indeed, as the situation continued, it was a disadvantage, following the introduction of auto-enrolment. Even a basic 3% employer contribution, over time, would have amounted to a reasonable sum. Initially, the inconvenience was seen as a compromise, where I could not take a big hit financially, and he could build the business up to scale.

Whilst on my six-month garden leave, naturally, I spent a lot of time think about how the business could research companies, and collective investment vehicles. Yes, I used to visit the office to see how John was progressing and discuss the future. But in this time, neither John, nor I, engaged to harm Brewin Dolphin. Neither did we attempt to poach their clients. John had his own relationships, which he had developed, and was very focused on navigating the Raymond James onboarding process. My view and experience of Raymond James was as a very poor business. I will expand on this as the book progresses. There were not many options open to John, so I would not blame him for choosing to work within their branch model. In addition to this, John, quite understandably, wanted to use his own trade name. Originally, Vertus Asset Management, but modified to Vertem Asset Management. This came after Raymond James identified a potential trademark infringement, which was spurious at best. Although, belatedly, I am not at all surprised that the FCA have taken issue with this business. They were, in my opinion, an awful business. The model was flawed. They promoted themselves as offering a home for independent wealth management businesses. However, in the same way as the appointed representative model in the IFA sector, the Raymond Names approach was fraught with risk, as it relies on remote compliance. They were trying to apply a blanket approach to a wide diversity of businesses. To compound the problem, their quality of staff was terrible. To avoid misunderstanding, this is not to suggest that John had anything other than the best of intentions for his prospective clients at this time. In my opinion, Raymond James treated him very badly, and he fought very hard to save, and then grow his business. I will return to Raymond James but will now pivot back to the formation of the Vertem Asset Management business.

John had enlisted the help of some students from Durham University. The idea being, they would get some experience along the way. They were good lads; we enjoyed some camaraderie. When I went into the office, John used to reward us with an occasional fry up at a café called The Townhouse, which is located close to Newcastle Central Station. One of the students, James Pauw, stayed with us. He had just completed his degree. I recall it being Biosciences. He became fascinated in what we were doing and changed his career plans. John somehow scraped together the money to take him on. It was a good decision. He was excellent. He with us for some years. He passed his exams and was always destined for better things. The business had moved to Jesmond when he left. Without getting ahead of myself, I remember thinking to myself he has made a good decision, despite being sad to see him depart. He moved to Blackrock in London, and then transferred to Hong Kong. In terms of colleagues, he was one of the best I encountered in my career. He invested in the business too. I am not sure if he saw any return on his investment. Towards the end of his time with the business, I am sure he had his doubts about John, but was too polite to articulate them. Moving back to the early days, we put James Pauw to work analysing the pharmaceutical and biotechnology stocks. He picked it up very quickly. He was always quick to learn, and also assisted John in many aspects. John was also analysing stocks, mainly covering the technology sector. He was very capable and enjoyed the process. Him and I also devised the asset allocation process. Our careers had taught us that correlation was a fair-weather friend, and we build flexibility into the process to accommodate such. We both very much enjoyed the intellectual side of the process. The three of us were cramped into a little serviced office, but it felt like home. We enjoyed the fact we had little resources, and always felt like we could take on the best. John was very different then. You could see he was animated in a positive way. He was very passionate about the business. I remember John and I going on a road trip to meet potential clients. We covered much of the south of England, including London, staying in Village Hotels. Sharing a room, as we were on a budget. We met colourful characters and had fun in the process. But despite our optimism, Raymond James never made it easy.

It was often said that when people break off and set up their own investment businesses, the assets collected undershoot initial estimates, and the process takes longer. In our case this was certainly true. Sadly, it was greatly compounded by the workings of Raymond James. The onboarding process was terribly slow. They never appeared to be candid with John. He would face obstacle after obstacle. We used to say like rabbits out of a hat. Just as he thought he was getting somewhere; more rabbits would appear. This was a big problem, as John had lined up IFAs who were willing to transfer discretionary investment clients. But they themselves needed solutions and could not wait for prolonged periods. It was not John's fault; I could see that he was trying his best. In addition, the Raymond James charging structure was not cheap. They charged for everything they could. John lost a few IFAs who wanted to use us, but could not hang on any longer, as the months slipped by. Fortunately, one company, Island FS, were very loyal to us, and were the founder client for the business. Duncan and Adrian Buck were very patient, and without them, the business would have collapsed. I remain very grateful to them both, as they placed their faith in John and I. It was not until around September 2010 that John managed to get the business properly onboarded. Given the slender resourced with which the business was established, this delay clearly stretched the finances. John appeared to maintain good relations with his investors, principally led by Harry Wilson. Harry also provided access to his accountant, Carol Dangerfield, to help the business manage finances. Their support was also vital, and I remain grateful to them all, given the risks I had taken in joining the business. With the onboarding process finally negotiated, the Buck's started to refer clients, although Raymond James was still proving to be awkward partners. Island FS are based in Buckinghamshire, I scarcely met them, but spoke a good deal with Adrian, who provides technical support for Duncan. Duncan had a good niche of clients in the marketing sector. I met some of the clients, and they were generally intelligent, and obliging. I was greatly appreciative of their business, and respected that they had taken a chance with a start-up asset manager. It was a great distress to me when it was brought to my attention by Adrian Buck, that some of the clients that helped us start the business, were caught up in the WealthTek administration. They were very loyal clients. This is not to suggest that I did not feel great sympathy for all WealthTek clients, be they associated with Vertem Asset Management, or third parties. It is a stark contrast to the beginning of the journey when John, James, and I, were desperate to do well for them. I look back fondly on those days. In addition to identifying a number of exciting direct equity opportunities, we had formed relationships with independent collective investment groups such as TwentyFour Asset Management, SVM Asset Management, and Revera Asset Management. I also recall we were early backers of Alex Savvides, at JOHCM. We were looking for earlier stage investment opportunities. We were not exclusively small cap, and boutique asset manager focused, rather than looking to leverage our flexibility, when suitable opportunities arose. I also had the opportunity to return to teaching at Newcastle Business School, which had an important impact of the development of the business. At the start of semesters faces were unfamiliar. It generally took a few weeks before I was more familiar with students, as I was part-time, and had generally never encountered them before. Students could see that I was a little different, also being a practicing investment professional. I enjoyed relating the teaching material, which sadly was not my own, to real life investment cases. After the first session with a group, I received an email from a student asking about some work experience. The student was James Flintoft. James had just started his second year at Northumbria University, and wanted to come in when his schedule permitted, to learn about how we worked. James played a major part in the development of the business and was the best colleague I have ever had in my career. This was my opinion up to the point of ending my association with Vertem Asset Management. Post this point, my opinion is naturally cloudier. He enjoyed visiting, and we enjoyed having him in the office. Even though he was a student, it was like he was already part of the team. We never demanded he come in, but we missed him when he was not with us. He hoped to complete his year placement with us, but the business did not have enough scale to afford him. Nevertheless, he was pragmatic, and proceeded with his final year, successfully completed his degree, and then joined up. I stepped ahead to place James's involvement in context. It is also worth considering the great pity of what became of Vertem Asset Management. My grief is nothing in comparison with the stress placed on the clients of WealthTek, post the special administration, however, my point is we once had an excellent, and strongly motivated team, which could have achieved so much more. When James started visiting us, we were still in the initial small office in Collingwood Buildings. I remember that first winter was very cold. We were working in coats for the first few hours of the day. John would bring in a coffee from the independent shop opposite, which help warm us up. We had some portable heaters, one stank of burnt dust, but the joy of working together, and our collective optimism, more than offset the cold. While the client numbers started to climb, one perennial issue was the Raymond James charging structure. They essentially used a white labelled version of the Pershing platform and overlaid it with their own charges. Dealing costs were very penal. The bargain charge was £27. That is a £54 round charge for a buy and sell. In the Barclays

Wealth and Brewin Dolphin worlds, there was always the potential for the less scrupulous to churn portfolios. However, the Raymond James structure almost created a disincentive to trade, as these charges were paid away. John was very much aware of this and did his best to absorb some of these onerous charges, so as clients were not disadvantages, and the trades placed were in their best interests. This again made life tough for him, and the business. Nevertheless, he worked tirelessly to grow the business, and while it was still early days, the portfolios were performing well, which pleased us all immensely. We were soon able to move to a larger office, within the same buildings.

The new office was more spacious. It was a pleasant corner office, with more light, and a view towards Newcastle Central Station. We were heading in the right direction, but marketing was tough. We were very reliant on Island FS. Duncan and Adrian remained very supportive, but if the business was to be sustainable long-term, the client base needed to both grow, and diversify. Harry and Carol visited us and were always supportive. I remember one point Harry made regarding growth. He alluded to the challenge of growing a business and maintaining its founding values. I understood his point, and his comments certainly echoed clearly throughout the years. At about this time, John offered me the opportunity to purchase some equity in the business. It did not seem the right thing to do, as I felt I was already taking a career risk. In addition, I was not impressed with Raymond James, who I considered to be an impediment to the growth of the business. Although I only saw him on a few occasions, Harry was always interesting, owing to his knowledge and experience. We exchanged a few emails, and recommended books to each other. One stands clear in my memory. History was taught very poorly at the schools I attended, but I have grown to see its value in adulthood. I recommended the book, Jabez: The Rise and Fall of a Victorian Rogue. The book features the exploits of Jabez Spencer Balfour, infamous for the scandal at Liberator Building Society. It was alleged that depositor funds were misused and channelled into his business empire. As is often the case, any potential wrongdoing aside, he certainly did not receive a fair trial. There was a good deal of corruption in the bankruptcy process, as some of the assets were very high quality. Investor protection schemes did not really exist in the late Victorian era. Ironically, Croydon Road, and Tamworth Road, in the Arthur's Hill area of Newcastle, both were constructed by his businesses. Jabez, never one for modesty, was the proprietor of the once famous Hotel Cecil, in London. Harry emailed me complaining that he found the book boring. Jabez provided me with the lens in which I came to view John's activities. As I write this book, John had not been charged, and but remained under investigation for the collapse of WealthTek. I respect this status. The theory I came to develop was just that, a theory. When it comes to fraud, the faces, and the instruments change, but the tricks do not. It essentially boils down to a person, or persons, dazzling clients with their own money. I often wonder if Harry remembers that email exchange. Briefly skipping forward, whilst I never held any suspicions that Harry and his investors were engaged in any wrongdoing, far from it, it did surprise me that they were so tolerant of John's management of the business in its later years. There were a few initiatives we tried to raise the profile of the Vertem Asset Management, and to generate business locally. Citywire were kind enough to feature John and I as cover stars, which we greatly appreciated. Little did I know that some years later, I would feature heavily in an article by Jack Gilbert, covering the staggering FCA failure, and the demise of the business under the WealthTek umbrella. We also contributed regularly to an online news platform, Bdaily. To put more of a face to the business, we organised some seminars, and enlisted some help from SVM Asset Management and TwentyFour Asset Management. We invited IFAs from the region, and hoped that collectively, we could generate some business. In one sense they were comical, and in another, they turned out to be very significant for the development of business. I can remember one was held at St James' Park. The Idea being, John and I would present on the Vertem Asset Management process and proposition, to be complimented by Neil Veitch of SVM Asset Management, and John Magath of TwentyFour Asset Management. I recall John Magath was also accompanied by a fund manager too. The night before, John and James Pauw had a heavy night out with the TwentyFour team. I did not join them, as I was ill, and tried to recover for the seminar. When I arrived at the office in Collingwood Buildings, I found John and James Pauw in a diabolical state. They were still drunk and stank like stale breweries. I could not with any credibility criticise them. I knew, had I not been ill, I would have been no different. John was so drunk that when he went for a cigarette outside Collingwood Buildings, he did not even notice the SVM Asset Management team, whom he knew well, entering the lift, as he was leaving. James Flintoft came over to help us, and the SVM team helped prepare the name badges, as I am not sure James Pauw could even see straight. Collectively, we made our way over to St James' Park, but it was clear that John could not deliver his presentation. The attendance was reasonable, and somehow, we got through it. I had to deliver John's presentation blind, but fortunately understood the investment case for the stocks he had featured. SVM Asset Management and TwentyFour Asset Management delivered their presentations very professionally. I remember Neil Veitch making an amusing comment about symposiums, I assume in the manner described by Plato in remembrance to Socrates. As for the TwentyFour team, who were always impressive when I met them, I can only assume that they are very durable professionals, as there were no signs of a hangover in their delivery. Perhaps not surprisingly, we did not generate any notable business from the attendees. However, it was a company that did not attend the seminar, which would have a very important role to play in the way Vertem Asset Management developed.

Shortly after the seminar, John received an apology for not being able to make the seminar from a company called InvestAcc, who are based in Carlisle. Before I proceed with the book, it is only correct to inform readers that at the time of writing, I was employed by Vesta Wealth, part of the InvestAcc Group. I want to be clear that this book was written independently, and represent my own views, and experiences. It is not to be considered as stealth marketing, or a promotion of any kind. Pleasingly for us, despite not making the seminar, they were keen to meet, to find out more about out services. John made contact and arranged for him and I to visit their offices in Carlisle. We were both very enthusiastic about the meeting. Unfortunately, I had a bit of a disaster prior to the meeting. I was teaching at Newcastle Business School at this time, and enjoyed using the facilities at Sports Central, particularly the squash courts. One lunchtime, James Pauw and I headed over for a game. James was technically far superior to me, but I was very fit, owing to running regularly, which helped reduced the skill deficit. We enjoyed competitive games. This particular game was no different. We were battling it out in the middle of the court, and as I turned, I took the squash ball fully in my eye. The pain was incredible. It was watering incessantly. I could not open it and felt disorientated. I was swearing and James Pauw was apologising. I remembered saying, I am swearing because it hurts so much, not because I blame you. It took a good while after to assure him there was no blame. He helped me stagger back to the Vertem offices, and I had to lay on the floor. I felt in pain and drunk. I took a taxi to the RVI Newcastle, fortunately they determined that there was no damage to my retina. I did, however, have a lot of bruising, and was advised to wear sunglasses, as my pupil was not reacting to changing light conditions. On the bright side, the consultant advised if my eye hurt, to go to sleep to rest it. This made the trip to Carlise a little tricky, as I had the appearance of being a brawler. My eye did not look good. Nevertheless, the meeting was important to us, and we headed over. I felt embarrassed, and upon meeting Nick Gardner and Jon Targett, tried to make a joke at my own expense to break the ice. Fortunately, they were very welcoming, and generous. We started to explain how the business was created, and developed, as a boutique asset management business, aimed at the IFA outsourcing market. Our target market being genuinely bespoke discretionary managed portfolios. John and I were caught slightly out of step, when it was explained that they were looking for an investment management business to design a suite of risk profiled model portfolios, for an internal centralised investment proposition. They did not want to partner with a larger national business, where they would be just another client. They were keen to work together. Whilst the meeting had taken an unexpected turn, John and I left enthusiastically. Many new businesses have to adapt to new situations. When we thought about what was required, it was a good opportunity. They wanted a suite of portfolios deigned to match Dynamic Planner risk outputs. Something that was not off the shelf. Something unique to their business. This was what Vertem Asset Management was designed to do, provide bespoke solutions for IFAs. It was just in a slightly different way than we had anticipated. After further meetings and dialogue, we designed a suite of portfolios that met the requirements of the business. It was convenient for InvestAcc for these to be managed on what is now the Fidelity Advisor Solutions platform. It was a very nice process. Both businesses enjoyed working together. There was trust. It was clear that they had a good approach towards their clients, which is very important. During our efforts to grow and diversify the business, we met many IFAs which were misaligned with our values. We did not want to grow at all costs. It was important to us to work in partnership, to deliver value for clients. In my career, I have been happiest when I have done well, because clients have done well. It is like completing a circle. Everything is in balance. When the relationship is out of balance, it does not end well. There was, however, one familiar obstacle to our promising partnership. Raymond James.

John approached Raymond James with the proposition and met with obstinance. They refused to allow the portfolios to be managed on another platform and would not yield on their charging structure. I could clearly understand their desire to monitor the suitability of the offering. This was their responsibility. We of course had no objection to this, as it was also our desire to ensure the offering was suitable for clients matching Dynamic Planner outputs. It would have of course been impossible to manage the portfolios within the Raymond James charging structure. Bargain charges of £27 each way rendered it impossible, as rebalancing exercises would be extraordinarily prohibitive. They would not compromise to accept visibility on the Fidelity platform, and the process used to manage the portfolios. This placed John in a very tight spot. A transformational business relationship, one forged on goodwill, with every intention of delivering a suite of portfolios to serve clients well, was being blocked. They had a grave lack of understanding of the market. John was asked, is this the sort of work you want to do? The business was being throttled by Raymond James. In reference to the US rock band The Eagles, we were in the Hotel California.

Checking Out and Trying to Leave

I have made my views on Raymond James clear. The company will no doubt see things differently. Life is about opinions. Even their compliance did not make sense. We had structured products rejected on the basis of potential capital losses. Oddly enough, the structures we wanted to use were volatility trades, with little risk to capital. We merely wanted an efficient way to exploit changes in volatility. At the same time, they were happy for us to invest in direct equities, which, as we all know, can result in a 100% capital loss. They did not take any interest in our process. We could have been picking stocks out of a hat, and they would have been none the wiser. Of course, we were doing no such thing, and were trying our best to find undervalued businesses. This did not mean that we were slavishly value styled. We were equally interested in undervalued growth. John had to find a way out, but it was very tough for him. One major obstacle was the trading name of Vertem Asset management. Legally, Raymond James owned it. Many things are open to interpretation, but it was difficult not to view this as pair of professional handcuffs.

John had to run the business, and also search rapidly for a way out. An alternative business to provide the necessary infrastructure, and regulatory umbrella, so Vertem Asset Management could achieve the growth it needed to be sustainable. In addition, John had to press ahead with the relationship with InvestAcc to manage the model portfolios on the Fidelity platform. Like most relationships, progress was sometimes a little slower than we would have liked, but the goodwill was strong on both sides. Goodwill prevailed, and the relationship came to fruition. There was a void. The management of the models fell between the transition. They were of course always managed in accordance with the mandate. In reality, John had little viable choice. I am aware that I lack both the eminence, and talent, to warrant an autobiography. In writing this book, I have tried to capture the context of both developments, and thoughts. I believe at this time, only a few years into the life of Vertem Asset Management, John was desperate for the business to succeed. He was also conscious of the careers, including my own, that depended on it. I respected this. As poor as I found Raymond James to be, in the context of what became of WealthTek, I do not believe any client assets were compromised. Again, I must respect that when writing this text, John faced no charges. In the context of the theory, I developed, which led to me raising concerns with the FCA, and others, a logical question to ask is did John intend to use the transition from Raymond James to misuse client assets? In my opinion, the answer is no. However, the theory I developed, and indeed still wish to be incorrect, believed the transition created the conditions for it to happen. The transition was messy. At haste, John needed to provide an alternative. There was not enough capital to take the directly authorised route. He explored a number of options. Some progress was made with Multrees in Edinburgh, which appeared to be a viable option. This was to end in disappointment, as John felt let down, as result of being deprioritised in favour of a larger client. This I cannot corroborate and relied upon his word. During his search, he came across the Sapia solution, which was headed up by two bright Germans, Gerhard and Jurgen. They were able to provide the regulatory architecture in a similar format to Raymond James. Vertem Asset Management being a trading name, but under less restrictive terms. John still needed to put together the rest of the infrastructure needed to run an asset management business. This became a big problem, as the business ended up functioning with a patchwork of infrastructure, that ultimately did not work very well. Nevertheless, amid these difficulties, the business was still making progress. Island FS were still referring good quality clients, and the relationship with InvestAcc was developing well. It is important to note that the model portfolios, being managed on the Fidelity platform, were never at risk. We had also made some progress with a few local IFAs. We had some meetings with Portland Financial in Jesmond. This is somewhat ironic, given the association between Ryecroft Glenton and Vertem Asset Management, which is significant in the context of subsequent developments. Tony and Peter Glenton are both very sharp, and no doubt have a good client bank. We reached the point where they were considering testing us with some of their more complex investment clients. Sadly, some nighttime chicanery killed the relationship at the concept stage. My friend, Mark Hutson, had spoken favourably about us to a local IFA, Laurus Associates. We had some meetings with the business, which were positive, and went on establish a relationship. They have a good client base. Most importantly, they have a good approach to their clients. They referred some good clients. As always, John managed the relationship. At that point in time, John managed the relationships, and operated as the portfolio manager. James Flintoft had joined the business full-time, so he, James Pauw, and I, worked as analysts. I worked as a dedicated analyst, while the two James's also assisted John with some administration. We were also joined occasionally by another former student of mine, Sahil. He was an accounting student, and I was the Associate Lecturer for the Corporate Finance module. He was excellent and has progressed to have a very good career in Corporate Finance. I met him for a lunchtime coffee in Newcastle, a few months after news of the WealthTek scandal broke. I am glad he took the right path with his career. Skipping forward, John let down and embarrassed Laurus Associates. Poor service destroyed the relationship, which was a great pity. It was sadly indicative of what a bad business Vertem Asset Management became. I am sure Colin and Karen look upon this as a very fortunate escape.

As John entered into his relationship with Sapia, he needed more personnel to cover the functions previously fulfilled by Raymond James. This led to his wife Jess joining. This made sense, as she had back-office experience with Brewin Dolphin, and no doubt arrived with knowledge and operational guidance. Jess was steady, and reasonably reliable. Beyond this point, John's recruitment was generally diabolical. He took on his friend, Dan, as a makeshift dealer. I have nothing against him personally, but he was the worst dealer I have encountered in my career. I do not write this lightly, as there were very indifferent dealers at Barclays, Brewin Dolphin, and Raymond James. My concerns rested with best execution. Trades were often left, somewhat slackly with market makers. We were working hard to find ideas and create profits for clients. I did not want to see these lost to slack dealing. There were other recruits who were also vastly unsuitable. I could never fathom his recruitment. It was not long before John was looking for an alternative office. The problem with serviced offices is you are hostage to your neighbours. Collingwood Building was full of indifferent occupants. The worst of all being the charity fund raisers. I found it hard to reconcile why charities entered into relationship with these odious businesses. I also remember a business offering courses Botox injections. They disappeared with many courses unfinished. It was like a scene from Benidorm, and not conducive for an asset management business, looking to establish professional relationships. After a period of searching, he settled on an office in Jesmond. The Gresham, a converted hotel of the same name. It was ironic, as my first flat in the city was on Grosvenor Road. It was actually a throw of a stone away from the carpark of The Gresham. The front and bottom part of the building was occupied by Pizza Express, which made us popular for lunchtime meetings. Vertem Asset Management would occupy the back, and top of the building.

Lost to the Races

I think John choose the office well. The office required some modification, but it was a good fit. Jesmond has always been an enigma. Locals regard it as posh and upmarket. If you gave this description to someone outside the UK, they would look at you with disbelief. It is a strange mix of desirable houses, and terraced slums. But sitting just off Osborne Road, The Gresham, by local standards, created a professional image. It should have been a happy move. For a brief period, it was. Being candid, I spent some of the lowest points of my life, and career, whilst working at The Gresham. To refer to the title of both the book, and chapter, I cannot precisely claim to know when John's interest in horse racing began. I was aware of it before the move to The Gresham. But it was whilst at this office that it really started to escalate. In many respects, he was made for the sport. If I can refer readers back to how John financed his investment to launch the business. He is an intelligent, numerate man, who can spot and opportunity, and his not afraid to gamble. I know next to nothing about horse racing, but I was not surprised that he was drawn to the sport and enjoyed success. I will also touch on the Sapia relationship. In the manner of the phases of the business noted above, this was the second. The Sapia relationship was much less of an operational straitjacket in comparison to Raymond James. Although, aspects of the relationship were dangerous. It was another example of distance compliance. There were other aspects, which were troubling. The relationship, at least initially, did not appear to be sufficiently arm's length. At a later date, Sapia moved its onboarding operation to Newcastle, which, for a time, was accommodated in The Gresham. It is very important that the relationship between the operational side of an investment business, is sharply demarcated from the compliance oversight. In retrospect, I came to see that the arrangements were not adequate. This appeared to compound the risks of a distance compliance relationship. I do not mean to insinuate that any company operating under the regulatory architecture of another is bad, but the risks are certainly more elevated. When the Sapia onboarding operation was moved into The Gresham, it did not appear to be a robust operation. Again, this is based on opinion. The local staff that they recruited were not individuals who inspired confidence. I often formed the impression that they were dealing with companies who had been turned down by multiple alternatives. Again, in retrospect, I could appreciate that Vertem Asset Management did not make the most of the operational freedom provided under the Sapia relationship, indeed it regressed, while the risks to clients increased. I will expand on these points as the book progresses.

The early stages of life at The Gresham were broadly positive. The relationship with InvestAcc flourished, and the models were progressing well. I always enjoyed our trips to Carlisle to present to the business. In similar fashion, our relationship with Island FS was strong. I always enjoyed talking to Adrian. Duncan delt predominantly with John. We were visited by John's investors, including Harry and Carol, and enjoyed a nice evening. I probably enjoyed it too much, as early the next morning, I travelled to Ibiza for a family holiday. Sadly, it was not long before deterioration set in. I will start with infrastructure. As I noted above, Raymond James, in my opinion, treated John very badly. The pressing need to transition away from Raymond James, to save the business, led to a horribly botched infrastructure, which ultimately sowed the seeds for its demise. My role continued to be as it always was, investment analysis. I never placed a single trade during my time of working with Vertem Asset Management. Neither did I have any interaction with the client management system. I had enough experience elsewhere in my career to see that it was wholly inadequate. Collectively, we could see that John was trying his best in a tough situation, and believed his perseverance would lead to improvements. There appeared to be major problems with reconciliations between the client management system, and assets held by custodians. It was assumed that these were teething issues, and quite possibly, initially they were. Consolidated tax reporting was being computed via an excel spreadsheet, invariably by John. Computing a tax position from unreliable information will never lead to a good outcome. Clients, and their accountants, began to notice the discrepancies. Performance calculations also evoked concerns. I had a causal glance at some valuations and could not reconcile the methodology used to calculate the performance of client portfolios. It was seemingly being calculated via excel, by John. It was not easy to get close enough to ascertain the credibility of the output. John was often furiously reluctant to delegate. This was closeted with the Vertem Asset Management is my baby narrative. At its core it was, that was toxicity to this mantra. He had unfettered access to all areas of the business. The front and back office. In addition, he had a very large intellectual, and experience, advantage over the staff he did delegate to. The most obvious examples being Jess and Dan. John sold the perpetual story of improvements. He appeared to maintain an ambition to create a more innovative alternative to Raymond James. To recruit more trading names, to sit alongside Vertem Asset Management, under the Sapia regulatory architecture. This he did with Malloch Melville. The infrastructure did not improve, if anything it got worse. He had a story to tell. I have used the frustrating experience of Raymond James, to create an architecture with Sapia, for dynamic forward thinking investment managers looking for a new home. Having been in that position, I can imagine it was a well-received pitch. By this time, he had begun to project an imagine of a successful businessman, rapidly making a name for himself in the horse racing world. The explosive increases in wealth were never easy to reconcile. John did not enjoy the strongest of credit records, owing past relationship difficulties. The financing of his house, the extensive renovations, expensive cars, and a property venture with Harry Wilson and his associates, were obvious examples. Nobody wants to believe that somebody they respected, and trusted, might be committing fraud. There was no definitive evidence. I wanted to believe it was down to his work ethic and savvy nature. Despite all that has happened, I still do. I could not at that time reconcile the person who created the business, with all the hopes and aspirations expressed above, with anyone who would contemplate the ultimate professional sin for an investment manager. I remained renumerated through the Collingwood Wealth vehicle. This was causing me concerns, as it was obvious faux self-employment, a matter raised regularly with Deborah Graham of Ryecroft Glenton. Deborah completed my tax returns from the creation of this ill-fated vehicle. She was aware of its purpose, which was a renumeration vehicle, and my interests in it stretched no further. Vertem Asset Management, under Sapia, was in a constant state of chaos. There was always something to be remedied with pressing need. Alongside this, John cultivated the image of a well intending, but chronically busy businessman. Be very wary of these instances, as they create the cult of exception. We really must get round to winding up Collingwood Wealth, and there are so many trade creditors calling because John is so busy to deal with the invoices, and so on. In cases such as WealthTek, you are likely to encounter the cult of exception. Why the key person plays by different rules and must be considered as a slightly eccentric alternative. This is part of their character, the part that makes them such a high achiever. Again, be very wary of this rhetoric. I took some comfort in the roles of Harry Wilson's accountant, Carol, the accountant to the Collingwood Wealth LLP, Deborah Graham, and audits conducted by Sapia, under Lawson Conner. I came to see that I was wrong. I am not suggesting any of these individuals engaged in wrongdoing. However, I came to see that humans enjoy the comfort of thinking in crowds. Some call this Groupthink. It is easier, and more comfortable, to take information that is readily available. I know from personal experience, that the cost of challenging appearances, and critically thinking beyond accepted thought, is high. Perhaps the fear of bearing this cost bestows too much goodwill on those that profit from such. I believe others fell into this trap too. There were a few early anomalies. I remember receiving a call from Gerhard from Sapia, querying a large amount of money that had been sent to Collingwood LLP. I recall the sum was a round £180,000, far beyond our immediate drawings. There was no indication from Gerhard that this money came from client accounts. Besides, he is a very intelligent, financially literate individual. I recommended he raise the matter with John, and requested he inform me if this was not resolved. I asked John about this, and he said the matter had been resolved. It was an oversight. This concurred with Gerhard, who was also satisfied. I also sought assurances from Deborah Graham, who in the course of completing our tax returns, was satisfied that Collingwood Wealth was not being used beyond its purpose. I also recall an unusual trade. It was a property fund that John had purchased for the portfolios, after attending a conference hosted by the asset management business. It was a unilateral decision, and not an output of our research process. It was his company, so he was able to take such decisions, and assume the associated responsibility. John was still operating in the portfolio management role at that time. I have touched upon the reluctance to delegate. I asked James Flintoft about this trade, as he had access to the client management system. In addition, we both asked John where the fund was held. He framed it as being held directly with the manager, as it was purchased during the transition from Raymond James to Sapia, which was a protracted process, as I have indicated. As time passed, and as clients started to leave the business, there was often a delay with the divestment of this fund. As an open-ended commercial property fund, this could on occasions be attributed to suspension periods, but not all the delays perfectly corresponded to such time scales.

Clients received their money, but the delays with this fund stayed with me. These instances could have been coincidental. I could have read them incorrectly. But they formed part of my later thinking.

The culture of the business greatly deteriorated during our time at The Gresham, despite the initial optimism. James Pauw left the business, which was the correct move for him. This gave James Flintoft the opportunity to take on more responsibilities. As both are very talented, the transition was smooth. Overall staff numbers expanded, due to the needs to support the operations of the business. It is unfair to say that all the appointments made by John were poor. Some were reasonable, if not outstanding. The days of recruiting people of the calibre of James Pauw, and James Flintoft, were well behind the business. John's recruitment ranged from friends and associates, to what appeared to be impulsive decisions. At the start of our move to The Gresham John was still engaged in the investment process. We held weekly stock meetings. But as time passed, John became absorbed in trying to run his fragile and dysfunctional infrastructure, along with other activities, which mainly involved horse racing. There was also a bizarre clothing venture, with a sub-Primark quality, to be sold at premium brand prices. Horse racing was by far the biggest distraction. The term lost to the races initially referenced the lack of focus in the Vertem Asset Management business. Later I feared much worse. As I referenced above, a focused John had a lot to offer the investment process. Him losing focus, and drifting away, was a big loss. In reality, when James Pauw left, and John disengaged, I could only rely on James Flintoft. Amid poor staff quality, and unreliable infrastructure, our concerns at this time related to client welfare. Not in the respect of the potential misuse of assets, but exceptionally poor service. We were feeding John investment ideas, but he was unfocused. Assets were invested in accordance with this overloaded schedule. There were large amounts of uninvested cash, and John would concoct a makeshift narrative about timing. This was often not credible as clients had missed out on potentially large gains. It became professionally embarrassing and was compounded by appalling administration. John ruined the Laurus Associates relationship, and eventually other clients started to leave. Even Island FS started to lose confidence. This was very sad, as they were founder investors. James Flintoft and I were trying to improve the situation, and had many meetings both between us, and with John, to institute such. The main obstacle was John's reluctance to delegate the portfolio management role. We would have incoherent meetings with him. I called them blue sky meetings. Positive change was always just round the corner. He maintained his first love of investment management and would return to fully engaged portfolio management duties as soon as operational issues were remedied. The corner was never turned. We did not want to oust him or dispute his ownership. We were stuck on a rudderless boat. Vertem Asset Management had become much worse than the businesses we set out to trounce. It was really hurting my professional pride, as clients were being let down.

Other than maintaining the hope James and I could institute improvement for the benefits of clients, I began to loath attending the office. It was more like a social club of John's acolytes. It was sickening to watch. As John's horse racing activities gained more prominence, he went on to remind me of Narcissus, and his self-admiration. He appeared to crave the cult of the microcelebrity. His office acolytes would trade off faux friendships, and admiration, for slackness. John appeared to have an obsession with recruiting a girl I used to teach at Newcastle Business School. She completed a year with Goldman Sachs, as part of her degree. I tried to tell him that she was nothing exceptional. She joined and was an absolute disaster. She was recruited to be his Head of Operations and structured her day around preparing meals to fuel her bodybuilding ambitions. I can recall many meal selfies. I tried to warn him about another student I had taught, Nathan. It was ironic when he mentioned he was interviewing a Nathan, whom I had taught at Newcastle Business School. For a moment, I was very enthused, as I had a student of the same name, who was absolutely outstanding. I tempered my optimism, as I felt sure this individual could go be recruited by a top investment bank. When I saw he was interviewing the other Nathan I taught, my hopes were dashed. He was a disaster for the culture of the business. My wife visited the office to take staff portraits for the website. When we returned home, she said I cannot understand why any investor who had built up wealth, would feel confident trusting it your colleagues. Sometimes, outsiders can make shrewd observations. Some colleagues would stroll in, and before they had even attempted any work, would troop over to Waitrose, opposite the office, to buy breakfast. They had barely done anything, and they were planning their visit to Tesco for lunch. Britain has a chronically bad issue with productivity. It is a complex issue, with many potential explanations. I used to follow the debate with interest. What that office taught is often the most overlooked explanations are simplest. People simply do not work particularly hard in Britain. Granted, that office was an extreme example, where I doubt many of them were working much over 40% capacity for much of the time. But it is a sore issue nationally. They were more interested in chatting, and spending money, rather than earning it. Some days the office felt like a parcel depot. The issue of casual dress is a contested point. However, in The Gresham, people dressed for leisure, and worked for leisure. There were days when there were major market developments, and only James Flintoft and I were discussing them. In the horse racing season, markets could exhibit any amount of volatility, and only him and I would show any meaningful interest. On a serious note, working in this office had a terribly negative impact on my mental health. As I covered above, mental health issues are underserved in society, and most particularly in finance. There is a feeling that there is no outlet because you fear for your job and career. It is a problem in the country too. Giving mental health almost parity with physical health, was long overdue. However, it opened up vast avenues for gaming. We are now at a point where disproportionate levels of scarce resources are allocated to those who see the advantage of using them, at the expense of those who really need support. It has opened up a new frontier of welfarism. Welfare in its essence is a positive force, but in Britain, its application has had a vastly negative impact on the work ethic of the nation. I was desperate to leave, but sometimes in life you have to place the needs of others above your own. This narrowed down my options considerably. I used to look at the calendar, and dreaded when James was on holiday. That equated to undiluted exposure to the toxic unprofessional culture. As for my own, I felt I could only take them in large blocks. If I could grind it out and have a two to three week break to look forward to, it was at least some salvation. Taking a few days here, and there, was never enough. I had to develop mental coping strategies. Firstly, I had to believe that even in this dreadful environment, if I remained professional, there was a chance I could do some good for clients. Other strategies were varied. Rather than listen to conversation infused with self-adoration, and shallow superficial nonsense, I thought I can learn something. If I were not talking to James, I would sit with my headphones, and stream history documentaries while I worked. Mentally, I felt at peace, and in another place. My day used to start with scanning the company news, identifying areas of interest, and circulating an observations document. This helped us identify new ideas, and, at least amongst James and I, to consider our existing positions. Depending on the volume of news, it entailed an intense period of concentration up to mid-to-late morning. To clear my head, I would take a short walk to a local Oxfam second-hand bookshop. I have always loved books, so this really lifted my spirits. I used to think of it as sifting around for unwanted knowledge. I now have a house cluttered with books, as when we reverted to homeworking, eBay became the substitute. One day, I found a book covering notorious events at Port Arthur, with a handwritten note, gifting the book, ten years after its publication, to Alexander the First of Yugoslavia in Christmas 1918. I imagine this must appear very boring and trivial, but believe me, it was a real pleasure in dark times. I also found refuge in exercise and wildlife. We had a shower at The Gresham. This helped, as I could take some exercise at lunchtime. Failing that, I would take my camera out and observe nature. I had a few favourite spots. One such spot was in Jesmond Dene. It was a little overgrown, but very private. I would choose this spot when I was particularly down. Often, I would be quite tearful. Knowing we should collectively be doing better, but not being able to improve it There was a robin which also frequented this spot. It used to sit very close and observe me inquisitively I wondered if the bird could read my thoughts. I felt like Dickon in The Secret Garden but lacked his oneness with nature. Simple moments of pleasure, some might term this therapy with nature.

In the search for new business, not even to grow, but to partially replace that lost via dreadful service, John recruited our old colleague, Vinay Bedi, as a consultant. The arrangement being he would introduce some high-quality clients and take an interest in the investment process. Without knowing what came to pass, I thought it was a promising move. Vinay has a lot of experience. This was most welcome, as John did not participate in the investment process, at this time. We needed more experience. Vinay did take an interest, as he was keen to ensure his clients investments were well managed. However, it was not long before he too encountered many of the shortcomings that had long frustrated me. Poor administration, John's lack of attention to portfolio management, and, by extension, his reluctance to delegate. With portfolio management decisions remaining hostage to John's schedule, collectively, James Flintoft, Vinay, and I, were able to persuade him that portfolio management should be delegated. This was met with reluctance, but we explained that unless he could give the role his full attention, we had a duty to express our concerns over the service provided to clients. We were not usurpers. I always made it clear that I would be delighted if he gave the role his full attention, as when he was fully engaged, I felt we were stronger as a team. James was the obvious candidate to move into the role. I felt more assured by this development, as we worked well together. I could pass ideas to him and know that they would be implemented efficiently. We used to attend many meetings together and enjoyed debating the investment cases. Even if the business were not progressing, I could be reconciled that remaining clients were well managed. There was another obvious advantage. This moved James far closer to operational side of the business. Next to John, he had the best oversight. He was the best placed to spot any wrongdoing that might be occurring. I encouraged him to focus very strongly on the accuracy, and timing, of income payments, along with corporate actions. I felt this would be the most likely places any discrepancies would be spotted. This is not to infer that he should have spotted any wrongdoing, only he was the best placed to do so. One of the major challenges would have been discerning any potential wrongdoing, from very poor administration. I later came to view this dynamic is a different way. There were compliance visits from Sapia, and audits were undertaken. A Latvian man used to periodically undertake audits. He had a professional appearance. However, I formed the impression that he was officious, rather than being intuitively intelligent. I have encountered a lot of compliance professionals, and investigators, who you could describe as educated, but not necessarily intelligent. This is no doubt a major factor why scandals keep occurring. People often play safe, and run with the herd, rather than taking the opportunity to challenge a situation. There is another factor that I should like to bring to the attention of readers. Vertem Asset Management had a five-star Defaqto rating for discretionary fund management. This was, of course, paid for. To my knowledge, nobody from the organisation even visited the office. Be careful of paid for ratings. The FCA will not have your back if something goes wrong.

I am not the best person to provide a narrative from the prospective of Malloch Melville. I am extremely sorry for what has happened to their business. They were an independent business, but I enjoyed interacting with Jeremy, Nigel, and Tom. They are experienced individuals, and in the office environment I have described, interacting and exchange views with Malloch Melville, was a bright spot. John's inadequate infrastructure, and poor back-office staff, held Malloch Melville back. I was amazed that they achieved what they did in the circumstances. In someways, I respectfully envied them. They were moving forward, while Vertem Asset Management was regressing. John was often slipping on promised improvements, and his administration team were so erroneous, that their efforts were often undermined. I suspect that because they had toiled so much, the thought leaving was too exhausting to contemplate. In this context, John's blue-sky talk was no doubt appealing. Again, the sheer number of administrative errors, would have been a great distraction from any possible wrongdoing.

When John announced that he planned to leave the Sapia relationship, and apply for direct authorisation with the FCA, wrapped up in one his blue-sky talks, it did not inspire me with a lot of confidence. It appeared to coincide with the intended sale of the Sapia business. I could of course be mistaken, but I did wonder if they were keen to derisk their business ahead of a sale. This was accompanied by plans to build his own platform, WealthTek. Even after more blue-sky talks, this did not make sense. John was often fond of applying fanciful valuations to his businesses. I remember one blue sky talk, when he even mooted giving James Flintoft and I some equity. This held little appeal, as I did not believe his investment business had any value. I could not see how it made any money. I thought back to my time at Webb Holton, which was at least an established business. The problem with Webb Holton, as noted above, was not growing the business enough. From what I could deduce, John was proposing create another business, alongside an existing operation that did not appear to have any value. I was never convinced about the alleged synergies between horse racing, and Vertem Asset Management. It simply did not make any sense. In one respect, it could be said that the commonality factor was wealth. A wealth management business, and a sport associated with the wealthy. But for me, it was a different type of wealth. I judged the horse racing sector to be more about punters. These individuals can be very savvy. Vertem Asset Management was about constructing, and managing, bespoke, discretionary managed portfolios, to achieve attractive risk adjusted returns over the medium to long term. This was alongside the model portfolios, which we designed to do the same thing, in the context of a centralised investment proposition. They are very different propositions. We were not speculating, or gambling. We were, at least I thought, investing. This was actually quite significant in my chain of thought. Managing an investment business is not easy. I have often regarded the FCA as an institution that regulates for its own convenience. They prefer a landscape of fewer, but larger, businesses. Fewer businesses to wave a stick at. You only need look at the life and pensions industry as an example. When I started my financial services career, there were a good deal more businesses than there are today. If you consider the workplace pension market, it is oligarchic in nature. In addition, you have the London Stock Exchange Group, a virtual monopolistic organisation, which is allowed to serially abuse its position. It grossly overcharges, particularly for information services. This greatly disadvantages smaller organisations, a factor that appears to cause little concern to the FCA. In this respect, the background of Nikhil Rathi, is somewhat concerning. The Continuing Professional Development (CPD) regime is also very penal towards smaller companies. Larger businesses can host CPD events, which is of course nonsense, as they are glorified sales pitches. They always want to educate on products and services they wish to sell. It is soft corruption. The professional bodies also do well out of this process. Developing markets, ready to receive UK financial services expertise, should take note.

With the Island FS relationship winding down, John appeared despondent towards the IFA sector. He presented a strange narrative for the reasons Island FS were pivoting away from Vertem Asset Management. I suspected that they were concerned about the direction his life was taking. At this point, I often wondered why he bothered with financial services. The Vertem Asset Management is my baby narrative did not appear overly convincing, particularly given his indifference to the investment process. If he could make money so much easier in the horse racing world, why bother toiling in financial services? The sport of horse racing is regulated, but I will leave readers to debate the integrity of this oversight, particularly, the financial elements. I have on occasion looked at the Titanium Racing Club and shook my head. I really could not understand the transparency, and governance of the club. Perhaps this was a function of my lack of knowledge. However, despite the ITV coverage, social media posts, and the robot, there were creeping doubts. The falling out John had with his previous trainer, and the ongoing chatter of unpaid debts, being examples. I have no involvement, or real knowledge of horse racing. Of the staff and associates of Vertem Asset Management, I was the most distant from the sport. Vinay was the closest to the sport. Nobody raised any real concerns, with the exception of one of John's largest clients. He called me one day and appeared agitated. I had met him and his wife on a few prior occasions and considered them nice people. He was very close to the horse racing world, had heard many rumours of unpaid debts, and was concerned about the safety of his investments. I explained that I was not involved in the operational side of the business, and that Vertem Asset Management was subject to regular compliance oversight by Sapia, which included independent audits of the assets. This was happening at the time. I suggested that he and John meet face to face to address his concerns. In addition, I suggested that if holding his investments with the business was causing him anxiety, it would be worth reviewing the situation. Naturally, I did not wish to see a very good client leave the business, but their welfare must come first. The idea of using a discretionary investment manager is to reduce stress, not be the cause of it. I informed John, and, as far as I was aware, the subsequent interactions between him and the client, addressed these concerns. As readers would expect, his concerns stayed with me. John is certainly a gambler, was he just pushing his activities to the limit? I also recall a conversation James Flintoft and I had at a Blackrock Investment Conference in Edinburgh, with an industry peer, who was also immersed in the horse racing world. His take on it was John really rolls the expletive beginning with f, dice. Beyond this, I could illicit no accounts of impropriety from the individual, notwithstanding my limited knowledge of the sport. I remember saying to James Flintoft, financially, I wonder if we all sit as hostages in John's casino. This, along with the appalling culture of the business, was fuelling my desire to leave. I was paid differently to the Vertem Asset Management staff. I was renumerated out of Collingwood Wealth LLP, and was reliant on John processing the payments on the last business day of the month. There were many payments which were late, although, I must state, that they were always made. I used to say to my wife that it feels like a hand grenade with its pin removed is being passed around, and I feared one day it would blow up in my face. I meant this in the context of John being the financial equivalent of Icarus. There was no smoking gun pointing to the misappropriation of client assets. I was certainly not close enough to the operational side of the business to find one. Returning to the point of the platform, WealthTek, I could not understand the investment case. At Vertem Asset Management, I wrote buyside research on diversified financials for over 10 years. The heterogeneous sector included businesses operating investment platforms. Some names will be familiar to readers such as Hargreaves Lansdown, AJ Bell, Nucleus and the Transact owner, Integrafin Holdings. In addition, there are others who are owned by private equity, or very large financial services businesses. My message here being it takes a lot of capital, time, and scale, to make an investment platform sustainably profitable. It is necessary to keep investing, as the functionality of the platform will begin to look tired. I doubted John could compete in this world from scratch, when his existing investment business operations were, in my opinion, worthless. It would have been lower risk, and easier, to partner with an existing platform, which could have been achieved at a relatively low cost. This decision returned to my thinking at a later point.

Nevertheless, alongside his increasingly media covered activities in the horse racing sector, John's ambitions for direct authorisation, and his platform, evoked interest. On the latter, I feel he was able to use the appetite for anything that could remotely be classified as FinTech. FinTech is a gross overused term. Finance is always innovating. Furthermore, an investment platform in an already competitive market, hardly stuck me as overly innovative. The previous infrastructure the business used was so poor, that the hurdle rate for improvement was very low. I was not involved in the build of the platform, but there were issues with the timing of its delivery, and financing. It was a very significant investment, and at one point, there was a standoff between the developer, and John. He was met with a demand for full payment or be left with an unfinished project. I cannot comment on the merits of dispute, as I was not close enough to the process. However, the financing of the project did remain with me as a curiosity. There was another factor that was part of the intrigue. John's shareholders, Harry Wilson, and his associates, were not keen on embarking on the journey to direct authorisation, due to the scrutiny this would entail. I do not believe there was anything untoward in their decision. I thought it more likely that they did not welcome the inconvenience. This meant that John needed to buy them out, to proceed with his ambitions. I was not privy to these transactions; it was my assessment that the business had little value. Valuation, particularly of private businesses, is highly subjective. The published accounts with Companies House, in microform, were essentially useless for this purpose, owing to time lapse, and their rudimentary form. I did wonder if John paid up handsomely for the shares, to keep up appearances. As shareholders, I was grateful for their support, particularly in the early days. Toward the end, their visits were well choreographed. There was little scope for interaction. If I had a criticism, it would be scrutiny. I wished, collectively, they had delved deeper. One interesting development came in the form of InvestAcc, who were keen to explore the option of the two businesses working closer together, particularly in the context of John's platform. I had long thought that in the right atmosphere, the two businesses were highly complementary. A combination would include pensions administration, wealth management, and asset management. A smaller version Mattioli Woods. James Flintoft and I were both enthusiastic about the talks. We both felt that any combination that might transpire, could introduce greater financial discipline, and oversight, as InvestAcc is a well-capitalised, and profitable business. A real business. I personally hoped any financial disciplined applied, would see a lot of waste cut from Vertem Asset Management. I never understood why several of my colleagues were employed. They showed little interest in the job, including gaining the requisite qualifications. John briefed James Flintoft and I about the talks and gave a bullish assessment. He suggested that some basic parameters had been agreed in principle, subject to further due diligence. I was cautiously encouraged but felt that John was vastly overstating the value of his business, but, nevertheless, in the context of the discussions, it was not my position to make that judgement. I judged the directors or InvestAcc to financially astute but was content to observe developments. As the weeks past, there appeared to be no progress. We asked John about the progress, and he suggested that the InvestAcc side lost interest. Dialogue had thus ceased. This is very significant for the events that were to follow. I settled back into the hope that the situation could yet be improved from within, or at least, failing that, client portfolios would be well managed. As we headed towards the end of the calendar year 2019, our focus was on positioning for the General Election. Living in the north of England, it was possible to deduce that Jeremy Corbyn, and his ambiguous position towards Brexit, was not being well received. We felt that Boris Johnson, and all his buffoonery, was going to win a comfortable majority, with his Get Brexit Done message. In retrospect, we came to see that it was more botched, than done. Nevertheless, portfolios were positioned for an unwinding of a potential Corbyn discount. This worked well, and I went away to Tenerife shortly after, felling reconciled that we had done well for clients. Returning in the New Year of 2020, I was soon met with the morale sapping, degenerate culture of the office. John was in better form, after receiving confirmation of direct authorisation with the FCA. This was not for me to question, as it had been a long process. However, approving his Head of Operations as Money Laundering Reporting Officer, a lady whose worth ethic, intuitive intelligence, and qualifications for the job, were not easy to determine, left a lot to be desired. I will return to this point later in the book. As John engaged in buoyant blue sky talk over his platform, and plans for expansion, it started to feel I was a resident in a Potemkin Village. Although the Potemkin narrative is dubious in its merits, its notoriety encapsulated my thoughts and feelings. Nothing made sense. James Flintoft and I were told not to worry about the regression of the Vertem Asset management business, as the WealthTek platform business would subsidise it, given its growth potential. This appeared to me as absolute nonsense. But shortly afterwards, the world changed, as Covid-19 arrived.

The World Changed

John, like other employers, was forced to adapt quickly to our new life of isolation. I remember the days prior to being sent home, I visited the Tesco and Waitrose stores in Jesmond to buy any durable foods available. Unfortunately, my grandparents had long passed, but it would be their generation who last saw shelves depleted so rapidly. The only difference between the two stores being the shelves at Waitrose were ransacked in a slightly more genteel way. I can remember the day we were sent home with a laptop. The students were having a last fling on Osborne Road, in Jesmond, for St Partrick's Day. As I walked to my front door carrying the laptop provided, the feeling came to me that I could never return to work at The Gresham. Aside from a brief blue-sky meeting with John, following James and I again expressing our concerns about the absence of a plan for Vertem Asset Management, my intuition was correct.

It was an extraordinary period, as readers will recall. Houses/flats were homes, offices, and schools. The stress was very intense. All my research required refreshing. It was not so much about the latest update, but more whether business could survive. I covered the financials, including real estate, so the workload was enormous. Alongside domestic responsibilities, I would often work until I fell asleep, usually on the floor. I was greatly concerned about permanent loss of capital for clients, should any of our holdings not survive. As a group, we started out by holding daily investment calls. When the situation settled down, we dropped the frequency. I did not take a day off until the Christmas period. It was all on James and I. It did not really matter whether the other analysts got out of bed and joined the calls, as their output was next to useless. John did not join a single call. James and I were largely abandoned with a team of weak, disinterested analysts. There is potentially a sad irony to this situation. I was worried to sickness about clients losing large amounts of money, and sadly, the same fate awaited them at a future point. Early in our period of isolation, John and I had a meeting with an adviser linked to Ian McElroy's Tier One Capital. It was a good meeting, as they were exploring options in the discretionary fund management market. It was left that John would send over some proposals for anonymised clients. I am not sure he ever progressed it, as I heard nothing more. I imagine they must look back with a considerable amount of relief. Vinay Bedi, to his credit, joined the great majority of investment meetings. His experience was useful. He was of course keen to safeguard the interests of the clients but was also content to offer his views for the benefit of all.

Just as we had weathered the worst of the market turbulence during the first lockdown period, and temporarily regained elements of our personal freedom, I received a disturbing call from James Flintoft. James had noticed that money had been flowing out of the model portfolios managed for InvestAcc, and now their newly created wealth management company, Vesta Wealth. John had long since given up any role, or interest in the management of these portfolios. They were managed by James Flintoft and I, with some administrative support from one of the other analysts. James had further noticed that they had created passive equivalents of the active portfolios we were managing. It was fair to assume that more money would follow in the same direction in the coming months. They remained by some way the largest client of Vertem Asset Management. James had received some feedback from the company to the theme of they had received discretionary fund management permissions and were tentatively building an alternative service. From the perspective of Vesta Wealth, this was eminently sensible. It is complimentary to run passive and active model portfolio offerings. There are periods in the investment cycle that play to the strengths of one over the other. In addition, I would imagine they had noticed that John's other activities were raising questions over to what extent he was devoted to managing an asset management business. In their situation, I would have no doubt thought about diversifying away from what were obvious distractions. There was also an earlier occasion when John had made an error in Judgment, which I always felt undermined the relationship. An adviser had left the Teesside office of the group and expressed an interest in continuing to use the models. John took the view that we should continue to offer him access to the models at his new company. This was a tricky call, because the models had been created for InvestAcc, who were our biggest client, and had been loyal in the process. John's view was they were not exclusive. My view was he should talk to Nick Gardner, given the importance of the relationship. This blew up in our faces, as InvestAcc became aware of what had happened, and the adviser switched away from the models, without notice, or explanation, after a short period. We had risked our best relationship for someone who showed not one ounce of loyalty. This issue aside, from the prospective of James Flintoft and I, the drift between the two businesses did appear odd, given that pre-Covid-19, they had tentatively explored the option of working closer together. A prospect that we had both welcomed. John's response to these developments was concerningly determinist. He provided a bizarre narrative that InvestAcc had likely used the talks as a factfinding exercise for their broader ambitions. Bearing this company was our biggest client, there was no coherent response to either stabilising the relationship, nor, what would replace the potential business losses. Besides, it was somewhat out of character from a business that we had known, and worked with, for many years. As Vinay Bedi had, at this point, already referred a number of good clients, there was no plan for Vertem Asset Management. No strategy. Only the previous line that the platform would keep Vertem Asset Management. The feeling of the Potemkin

Village came back to me. I had at this point, very much started to envy Malloch Melville, as they reminded me more of what Vertem Asset Management started out to achieve. Despite the many setbacks that John had created for them, they were working away and making progress as a boutique asset management business. Whereas we, at Vertem Asset Management, had become a sideshow for the infrastructure that was supposedly being created to help us grow. The tail was wagging the dog. I wanted to work with a business that was sustainable in itself, not one that was to be theoretically subsidised by a related entity. Particularly, when I did not believe the blue-sky rhetoric behind the WealthTek platform. I could not understand why anyone would seriously consider using it, when it only had a glorified landing site, rather than an impressive website. Only those carrying out shoddy due diligence would be persuaded.

James and I remained busy ensuring the portfolios, model and discretionary, were managed correctly, but nothing improved in the Potemkin Village. In the context of homeworking, we had become like the pawns of Pyongang, in the YouTube documentaries covering closely supervised visits to North Korea. Yes, everything is wonderful, our Supreme Leader is so wonderfully clever and so on. Something had to change. To quote my earlier example, the pin had been out of the grenade for a longtime. I was concerned that it was going to blow up in my face. James and I decided we would send an email to Nick Gardner at InvestAcc/Vesta Wealth, to try to understand what had really gone wrong with the relationship. A virtual meeting was arranged. We received a completely different narrative over how the aforementioned talks had progressed. It was explained to James Flintoft and I that some preliminary parameters had been agreed, leading to the need for due diligence, to support John's assertions over the value of his business. This is of course a normal process in business discussions. However, it was explained at this point, John did not respond to these customary requests, and did not answer any subsequent attempts at communication. We compared this with the narrative provided by John. I think both sides were surprised. Although, for myself, I was not surprised to be surprised, if that makes any sense at all. Very rapidly, my mind took me back to an occasion in the second office that we occupied in Collingwood Buildings. I remember Jess saying to John, sometimes it worries me how easy you find it to lie. In the context of the time, I interpreted this to have been half said in jest, but with meaningful undertones. Yes, many things are open to interpretation, but flipping back to the conversation of the moment, I believed Nick Gardner over John. This was a matter of personal judgement. Besides, what possible incentive would he have to be untruthful, they were still our largest client, and he has a successful business, while James Flintoft and I were working for an organisation in decline? As part of the conversation, James Flintoft and I were asked if we would consider working for the Vesta Wealth. There was a lot to think about at this point, so a further call was arranged. There were mixed emotions. There was the opportunity to work for a real business, rather than dwelling in a Potemkin Village. However, James Flintoft and I had spent a large part of our time analysing direct equities. We both enjoyed this aspect. But this comes with a good deal of responsibility, as equities can result in complete losses for clients in extreme circumstances. This is far less likely to happen with funds. Because of this asymmetry, it could certainly be argued that our meagre reliable resources, which were essentially ourselves, had become lop sided. The rump of the assets undermanagement were in the model portfolios, even after their shrinkage, but more time was spent on direct equities, for the reason just discussed. I suspect the InvestAcc side were aware of this dynamic. Direct equities are interesting to analyse, particularly in the mid and small cap areas, where coverage is thinner, and opportunities to find mispriced companies are higher. Essentially, with model portfolios, you are expressing more of your views via collective investment vehicles, rather than direct stocks. But this does not make managing model portfolios dull, as you still have to cover a lot of areas, including macroeconomics, alongside a multitude of asset classes, and subsections within them. Giving up full time analysis of direct equities is something I knew I would miss, but could also learn more, and build broader knowledge across the investment universe. I think with James Flintoft being younger, it was at this time, harder for him to see the situation in the same way. However, ironically, he has gone on to do the very same. There was of course another very serious aspect to consider. Having accepted the InvestAcc account of the talks over John's, we needed to confront another reality. This would mean that John failed to provide even elementary due diligence to the largest client of Vertem Asset Management, which sent an alarming message. It would not have surprised me that after appropriate due diligence, respective valuations were too polarised to justify moving forward, particularly as I was myself sceptical about John's perceived value of his businesses. In addition, as we know, valuing private business is a very subjective judgement. However, to not provide any due diligence at all, and not responding to communications, was another matter entirely. We can all at times overcomplicate life. But if a person, organisation, or institution, evades providing information, it is invariably due to a great reluctance to show it. I suggested to James Flintoft that this was very bad indeed. We had a further meeting with InvestAcc/Vesta Wealth, and afterwards James Flintoft decided he did not want his career to develop in a different way. He did not want to give up on direct equities. This was a tough juncture, as I very much enjoyed working with James Flintoft, and would have like to continue doing so. I suggested we take some time to consider. James Flintoft drafted an email to Nick Gardner, thanking him the opportunity, but it was not what we were looking to do with our careers. Nick Gardner replied in polite fashion, accepting the decision, and expressing some respectful disappointment. John's failure to provide rudimentary due diligence, and the snub thereafter, along with the different account we had been given, weighed very heavy. I felt that this was a pivotal moment in my life. The grenade without a pin was still be passed around, and now looked a good deal more menacing. I replied back to Nick Gardner, and explained that James had taken a different view, which of course he was entitled to do. I accepted an offer to join Vesta Wealth. I felt very sorry that I had broken from him but saw the loss of day-to-day analysis of direct equities in shallower terms. I did feel very emotional when I talked to James Flintoft about my decision. I explained my circumstances, and concerns that something was potentially seriously wrong with Vertem Asset Management, and by extension, WealthTek. I think he understood. Essentially, we saw the risks and rewards of the situation differently. This happens in life.

The next task was communicating my decision to John. This I did at the end of April 2021. We were still working remotely at the time, and John was often very busy. His list of ventures was growing ever longer and included the WealthTek platform and the move to new offices. I never visited the new offices, which were subsequently subject to the raid in April 2023. It was an unusual situation. I was not resigning from Vertem Asset Management, nor WealthTek. I was resigning from Collingwood Wealth LLP, that vehicle that I had long hoped would be wound up. I was resigning from a vehicle that was supposed to exist purely for the purposes of being renumerated for providing services to what was then WealthTek. I had no contract, and thus no notice period was stipulated. I emailed John, explained my decision, and suggested a one month notice period. He emailed back, politely, suggesting we discuss his plans, and to not worry about declining assets undermanagement, as the platform could carry the Vertem Asset Management, until it was revived. I did not want to be subsidised by a platform, and as I have noted, did not believe it was capable of doing so. Furthermore, I was very doubtful that Vertem Asset Management could be saved, as it would have been like try to restart a startup. I felt that its reputation had been impaired, and too many bridges burned. I replied to John, and suggested while he could attempt to revive Vertem Asset Management, I felt my journey was at an end. We agreed the one month notice period, and Vesta Wealth also served notice to bring the outsourced model portfolio service relationship to an end, with the same duration. I approached my last month with the same mindset as all those preceding it. I wanted to ensure all the research was up to date, and James Flintoft was fully briefed on all the positions held that were attributed to my output. It was important to me that client portfolios would be managed properly. John saw that I was still working hard but emailed and graciously suggested that I take a rest for the remainder of the month. Shortly afterwards, I met James Flintoft to hand back my company laptop. We bought a coffee and wondered around Little Moor in Newcastle. I understood that he himself had made a tough decision by remaining. I did not wish for him to be embroiled in any wrongdoing and reiterated that I felt potentially something was very seriously wrong. I was very sad to leave, as I had once held so much hope in Vertem Asset Management. Leaving felt like an admission that it was going to fail. Regarding any potential wrongdoing, I explained that I wanted to take some time to think it through rationally, outside the businesses. Removing the emotional attachment of working with the business. It is a very big move to suggest a person with whom you have worked with for many years, is potentially involved in fraud. Despite occasionally experiencing push back when discussing concerns over the running of Vertem Asset Management with senior colleges, and inferences that my negative views could be influenced by jealousy of John's success, this was never the case. I have acknowledged that he is intelligent, entrepreneurial, and possesses a sharp eye for an opportunity. I had no issue with the large gap in our respective material positions. As long as success was being achieved legitimately, I wished him well. My only concerns were his expressions of success, in such ostentatiously material form, was a shade disrespectful to clients. Clients desire relationships with successful people, but excessive expressions of wealth, in this case most pertinently in the form of luxury cars, could be seen in a negative way. Personally, I thought in the way of the ancient Greeks, nothing in excess. I must admit to sometimes thinking back to Ward Evans, their luxury fleet, and how that situation ended. I am not sure they could compete with John's portfolio of cars. No doubt, to my cost, I have always valued knowledge higher than materialism, therefore, the jealousy angle could not in any way be justified. My departure, did however, exposure a compliance shortcoming. In terms of the analysis and portfolio management function, only James Flintoft and I could realistically have been considered qualified and competent. John had not played any serious part in the investment process for some time. Vinay was a consultant, who joined stock selection meetings, but was not himself part of the process. Ordinarily, serious questions should have been asked about the strength of the team, with only one qualified and competent member. The problem being, John had oversight for compliance, and his assistant-cum Head of Operations, Catherine Hart, later O'Sullivan, was the money laundering reporting officer. I do not believe that Caterine would have knowingly engaged in any wrongdoing. I did subsequently wonder if she had been cynically used as a patsy. In all senses, John had complete control. With that in mind, nobody was in place to ask the necessary questions. It was the perfect Potemkin Village, as it even came with the approval of the FCA. The regulator has stumbled into the role of Potemkin Village idiot.

Before progressing to my thought process, I will make some further points about John. I wanted to write this book in a balanced way. Again, nothing I write is intended to disrespect the enormous stress experienced by the clients of WealthTek, nor other stakeholders, not least Malloch Melville. I never found John unpleasant to deal with. He was usually friendly and fair. I never asked John for be pay rise, but he did, over time, increase my payments substantially in recognition for my work. There were many occasions that I had to chase him for payments, but he did, sometimes with a short delay, pay. I am sure at this juncture readers are asking themselves, have I subsequently asked myself questions over how my payments were financed? The answer is yes, of course I have. I do not have access to the data to determine the answer. Needless to write, the thought of any of it being financed from client holdings makes me distraught. I can also state that this never formed part of my thinking when I reported my suspicions. I can also state that however disappointed I was with some former associates at Vertem Asset Management and WealthTek, I do not believe that any of them would be anything other than horrified, if any parts of their salaries were funded from client assets. Obviously, a financial services business is funded from charging fees and commissions to clients. What I mean is anything that was not legitimately contractual. I do recognise that some of my former associates may have found themselves disillusioned as there was little to no structure to their careers. They may have felt like they were cut loose, as in retrospect, it is possible to view their roles as potentially little more than passive actors in a fraud. I know from my own experience; it is mentally very difficult when there is little to no interaction with an employer. John also allowed me to work from Poland in some summers for several weeks. I appreciated this flexibility, and I believe he could see that I was productive in this time. Nevertheless, I was grateful. In September 2018, John paid for James Flintoft and I to take part in an investor tour of China. It was organised by Muzinich, over a one-week period, incorporating stays in Hong Kong, Shenzhen, Shanghai, and Beijing. There were many company meetings in the process. James Flintoft and I approached it in the right way, we soaked up as much knowledge as possible, to enhance our understanding of the Chinese economy. We did not approach it was a jolly and were respectful at all times. There was a bit of ambiguity in the status of our visa, which caused us a bit of concern. We were advised by Muzinich to apply for tourist visas, which was hard to explain when we visited the Visa Centre in Edinburgh. We were tourists visiting businesses, which appeared to have some overlap with a business visa. The latter would take longer to secure. Nevertheless, we negotiated this ambiguity, and secured our tourist visas. This played on James Flintoft's mind. I remember when we had finished up in Hong Kong, and prepared for the crossing to the mainland, still dressed in our business suits, James Flintoft disappeared. I was making a call to my wife, and suddenly he reappeared in casual attire, to look more like a tourist. I believe he thought the rest of the party, dressed in business attire, were fair game. I said to him if we are all detained, where do you think you will go? It did make me laugh. The border crossing at Shenzhen was through, but successful. I would also like to reassure our Chinese hosts, who treated us with respect at all times, that we merely enjoyed broadening our understanding of their economy, and nothing nefarious was attempted, nor ever contemplated. With that light-hearted digression aside, again, I have thought back to how the tour was financed. I would be mortified to learn it was funded inappropriately. I sincerely hope this was not the case. I reiterate that my motives towards John were never malicious. I always wished to be proven wrong. I would gladly apologise for holding such doubts if the shortfall in assets were recovered in the context of a giant misunderstanding. It is more accurate to write that I felt we had lost the John who had created Vertem Asset Management to the races. This was merely my opinion.

A New Start

My association with Vertem Asset Management, and WealthTek, via Collingwood Wealth LLP, ended on 31st May 2021. I commenced my employment with Vesta Wealth on 1st June 2021. The first month was especially busy, as I needed to put in place a research structure for the management of the active model portfolios. At Vertem Asset Management, this was not well documented, mainly due to the lopsided dynamics noted above. This is does not suggest that funds held we not researched, more that this needed to be better documented. I would also remind readers that the model portfolios, being managed on the Fidelity platform, we never at risk of any client asset shortfalls. In addition, my new colleague Matt, and I, wanted to streamline the range of portfolios offered, to make them more relevant to the advisers within the business. I took a two-week holiday to Poland in early July 2021. This provided me with the opportunity to think through thoroughly my concerns, away from my past associations with the business.

The process was an amalgamation of all the thoughts expressed in this book. I began by thinking about my former colleague, Mike Bains, and whether John might have taken the same erroneous path. It certainly appeared possible. There was an obvious disinterest in the business, and by extension, clients. As noted above, I found myself thinking of Narcissus, and his reflection, along with the ingratiating acolytes of the office. The cult of the micro-celebrity. He appeared addicted to this lifestyle, and the gambles taken to sustain it. Then there was the matter of finance. Could John be a contemporary equivalent of Jabez Spencer Balfour, with WealthTek playing the role of the Liberator Building Society? This also seemed possible. There had been explosive increases in wealth. Access to finance was surely difficult, due to past difficulties. There had been frequent calls from trade creditors, and there were stories of unpaid debts in the horse racing world. In addition, his portfolios of LLP's showed signs of distress, in the form of strike off notices. Looking at John's businesses from the outside, it was hard to see any value. What about the platform, WealthTek? The business case looked very unconvincing, as the industry is about scale, and pricing. He was up against competitors with far superior assets under administration, and deeper pools of capital. It did not make sense. Then there was the Potemkin Village, that had entranced even the FCA. Vertem Asset Management made no sense, it was going backwards at an alarming rate, and had just lost its biggest client. The website claimed to be manging approximately ten times the actual assets under management after I left. The narrative of it is my baby, I will never close it, appeared to be just another angle of the Potemkin Village. Sadly, after I left, there were a lot of Potemkin Village idiots, including the FCA. John's lifestyle of horse racing, nightclubs and fintech, should have raised serious alarm. Vertem Asset Management had just lost its most experienced associate in the context of the investment process, and nobody had raised a concern. This was a reflection of the Potemkin Village structure sanctioned by the FCA, where John was policing his own affairs. There was also the issue John's reluctance to provide even the most rudimentary due diligence to InvestAcc. The equivalent of asking to look behind the panels of the mobile village. I also considered the role of Collingwood Wealth LLP, which had extended well beyond its initial purpose. It was never the right time to wind up the vehicle, and I had expressed concern about the position of faux self-employment. Providing services to only one organisation. There was the strange payment, clarified with Gerhard from Sapia. In addition, during our period isolation, one of my associates at Vertem Asset Management, mentioned that when he was initially engaged by John, he was paid out of Collingwood Wealth LLP. After lobbying John, he was moved onto the company payroll. This was beyond the role of Collingwood Wealth LLP. This made we wonder if the LLP had been used as an off-balance sheet vehicle, to hide costs, falsify regulatory filings, and perpetrate fraud in the framework of the Jabez Spencer Balfour model.

I looked back on the evolution of the business. I began to fear that John, who I have acknowledged is intelligent and entrepreneurial, with a sharp eye for an opportunity, had, at varying points, been frustrated by a lack of capital, but gave in to the temptation of having access to capital. The dysfunctional infrastructure of the Sapia period, along with his control of the front and back office, would have made this possible. He had an enormous intellectual advantage over his acolyte staff. I thought it might be possible that he began with the mindset of borrowing client assets, with the intention of returning the capital, at a future point. I recalled the strange property fund trade, and pondered if he was using securities prices as a lending rate. Replenishing them when required. If he had taken this path, it was the moral equivalent of crossing the Rubicon. There was unlikely to be a way back. The departure of from Sapia was a mystery. Could it be possible that the intention to build a platform, was due to the desire to cover existing shortfalls? Transferring to a reputable platform would have triggered an audit, which risked exposing potential shortfalls. I then wondered if client assets had funded the building of the WealthTek platform, to cover their own shortfalls. In addition, was it possible that attracting new assets to the platform, could be used to cover existing shortfalls? A very dark picture was emerging. It was, however, only a theory. I wanted this theory to be incorrect. I still do. I was alone in my thoughts. My fellow senior colleagues held no concerns. They did not have the intuition to check behind the panels.

There were potentially two grizzly realities. Client assets were at risk, and I was being fitted up for a fraud, by an unwanted association with Collingwood Wealth LLP. I decided to raise these concerns with the LLP accountant, Deborah Graham of Ryecroft Glenton, the FCA, and HMRC. The FCA were contacted via the whistleblowing email address. I wrote to each, outlining my concerns that Collingwood Wealth LLP may be part of a wider fraud, which involves the assets of the clients of WealthTek. In essence, the LLP could be a conduit for settling the personal transactions of John. This was in July 2021. Deborah Graham emailed me about my tax returns, and also stated that all other transactions with Collingwood Wealth LLP were accounted for by John's drawings. I raised further concerns with her, by email in later months, however, these were ignored. She is well aware of this. These emails have been shared with the FCA and others. The FCA acknowledged my email later in July, and dialogue continued sporadically until November 2021. In November 2021, I was asked to complete a template, which I did. I received a reply thanking me for the information. No further requests were made by the whistleblowing team, or as they are referenced, the intelligence department. The latter being a somewhat creative term. My emails have been shared with The Times newspaper, and others. HMRC gave no meaningful acknowledgement. At this point, I had run out of options. Neither the FCA, Deborah Graham, nor senior associates at Vertem Asset Management, shared my theory. I remained unconvinced but would have been more than happy to be proven wrong. This remains the case. I concentrated on my current job. When I leave a position, I do not tend to look back. I do not spend time surveying former associates. I look forward, not back. Despite this, a number of colleagues and industry associates would, in unsolicited fashion, provide updates about John. It was usually those who monitored him on social media. It was none of my business, but, of course, a sceptical internal voice remained. Most people believe what they read and try to be hindsight geniuses. Comments then change to I always thought it was not quite right and so on. That, I am afraid is our society. Devices get smarter, artificial intelligence get savvier, but humans get dumber. The philosophers and the intellectuals have been usurped by uncouth celebrities and influencers. The latter terms being a euphemism for a grifter. Alas, we need not look any further than our smartphones.

April Sours

It was the morning of the 6[th of] April 2023, that I received a message from Jon Robinson of Ninety One, pasting in the FT article, covering the Special Administration of WealthTek, overseen by BDO. As noted above, I had spent no time looking back, and knowledge covering John's high-profile investments in the horse racing, and leisure sectors, had come via former, and current associates. On the issues of The Lofts nightclub, I did find myself on occasions wondering if stars such as Pete Tong and Idris Elba had, unwittingly, been paid out of WealthTek client assets? I can only hope not. The logical question at this time is, how did I feel on the receipt of Jon's message? First, great sadness, as I felt that innocent WealthTek clients, and other stakeholders, were going to suffer. Second, I felt exceptionally disappointed with the FCA, who could have intervened at a far earlier stage. Third, and also very sadly, I was not surprised. In fact, I was only surprised that it had taken so long. I felt that I had been cast as the jealous, estranged, co-founder. Unable to come term terms with our respective status in wealth, and profile. I had lost count of how many former, and current associates, who hailed John's apparent success and achievements. This, quite amazingly, included the WealthTek platform. That is the way our society functions. People long to be associated with success. Very few stop to question it. Social media has supercharged these inclinations. I also received a number of messages. Some senders had remembered my scepticism. But these feelings aside, there was no pleasure. I still wanted to be proven wrong, as this would save clients a lot of pain. Of course, the converse of these emotions was grave disappointment with John if my inclinations were correct.

After a short-period, I emailed the FCA, again via the whistleblowing address, stating my absolute disappointment in their lack of action. Ironically, it was the same lethargic individual with whom I had liaised during the process noted earlier in the book, who replied. It would be unfair to name him, as I do not believe it was the fault of one person. It did, however, demonstrate that the FCA had not acknowledged the catastrophic failure of its intelligence function. There is much worse to come on this. Their response was lamentable, and symptomatic of an out of control, arrogant, and unaccountable institution. These are strong words, but as the book progresses, readers will understand why. It is my great hope that this book helps to instigate serious reform. Reform beyond just the regulator. I was channelled down a cut and paste complaints procedure. A cul-de-sac. Nobody contacted me with an apology, and suggested a way we could work together to ease the stress on clients. Let us not forget, at this stage, clients had their portfolios frozen, and had scant guidance. It was a terrible moment. I had been met with mere callous institutional indifference. As a society, I feel it is time people took a stance against cut and paste responses, from those who let us down.

The next notable junctures were the Joint Special Administrators' report and statement of proposals, dated 30th May 2023, the FCA opening a criminal investigation into WealthTek and John Dance, closely followed by the now infamous 'Do the right thing' speech by Therese Chambers, Joint Executive Director of Enforcement and Market Oversight, published on 1st June 2023. At this point, I will focus on the latter, as it is very important in the context of this book.

Unpacking the Chambers statement, I could see exactly how the FCA were setting themselves up, and why we keep experiencing scandals in the financial services sector. Chambers, with the help of the notorious Dick Francis analogy, demonstrated how the FCA were seeking to control the narrative. It is what I called the French Revolution, or time zero approach. In terms of the former, I mean year 1 of the first French Republic. It is possible, that when this speech was delivered, Chambers did not know about the missed opportunities for earlier intervention. It is not easy to accept this possibility, but neither can it be ruled out. If she did not know before, she would have known very shortly afterwards. The latter, I can be assured of, as I complained to the FCA, reminding them that the narrative that they had acted to swiftly to safeguard client assets, was false. In their parlance, the FCA had made a false and misleading narrative, to both the general public, and the clients of WealthTek. In light of such, I suggested that they issue an unreserved apology to the clients of WealthTek. My request, as with any subsequent attempts to ask them to consider the human costs of their failures, was met with complete obfuscation. Chambers, as an experienced professional, at this point, should have needed no invitation to personally apologise. This is where we start to encounter our first issues with this case. The FCA, as a regulator, does not hold itself to the same standards as those it regulates. We have a moral vacuum. If a person, or organisation, were to issue a false and misleading statement, they would be liable to regulatory repercussions. At the very least, they would be expected to apologise to their clients, and issue the necessary clarification. At this point, both Chambers, and the FCA, lost their moral authority. I will now return to the time zero approach. The FCA are well drilled in this approach, some readers will have encountered it before. By setting time zero at April 2023, the FCA were seeking to control the narrative, articulating that they had acted swiftly to safeguard the assets of WealthTek clients. This, we know is untrue. Let us take my own example and consider it. When I contacted the FCA, via the whistleblowing address in July 2021, they were slow and ponderous, alongside displaying a lack of understanding of the significance of the risks brought to their attention. I raised a number of issues. First, the risk that Collingwood Wealth LLP was being used as part of a wider fraud, along with a recommendation to audit cash movements between the regulated entity, and other accounts, and vehicles, controlled by John. Similar to the work subsequently conducted by BDO. Second, I was concerned that Collingwood Wealth LLP had been used to hide some of the costs of the regulated entity, and thus potentially facilitate false regulatory filings. Third, embellished claims of assets under management. After I ended my associated with the business, and the management of the model portfolios transferred in-house to Vesta Wealth, the website was claiming to be managing fantasy levels of assets. This was providing clients, potential clients, and advisers, with a false and misleading impression. That said, Chambers went on to adopt a similar strategy for the FCA in her "Do the right thing" speech. Chambers has herself, failed to do the right thing, and apologise for this misrepresentation. Other issues raised included concerns over the remaining competency within Vertem Asset Management, in the context of the investment process. In my opinion, only James Flintoft was competent, after I ended my association with Vertem Asset Management. John had not been involved in the investment process for some years, and Vinay was a consultant, and was not writing research. Earlier in the book, I covered the dangers of distance compliance relationships via trading names, and how the FCA has, somewhat belatedly, woken up to the risks. I also reviewed the direct authorisation process, where the FCA were content with the Potemkin Village structure, with no independent compliance oversight, and a money laundering reporting officer who lacked obvious experience. If there is no independent compliance function, checks and balances do not exist. Some readers may recall that there were concerns raised about the relationship between Neil Woodford, and his compliance staff. I would encourage readers to be very careful here, and to ask companies they current deal with, or are considering engaging, to explain the independence of the compliance function. They failed to check behind the panels of the Potemkin Village. During the whistleblowing process, the FCA failed to connect even the most illuminous of dots. The most experience person within the investment process at Vertem Asset Management, a person involved at outset, had left the business, and raised concerns. In addition, some basic searches should have raised the alarm. John's coverage in both social, and more traditional media, suggested that he had been making large investments in the horse racing and leisure sectors. Furthermore, his lifestyle was not consistent with a person showing dedicated commitment to running a financial services business. A quick look on Companies House showed that reporting within LLPs was on occasions overdue, and subject to strike off action. If, collectively, all these factors were insufficient to warrant immediate attention, the use of the term intelligence in this function of the FCA, is disingenuous. They once again failed to check behind the panels of the Potemkin Village they approved. During my interactions with the FCA, I asked them to consider the crass Dick Francis reference. I deduced that Chambers enjoys detective stories. This is somewhat ironic. I ask readers to think of their favourite detective stories. I am willing to bet the central character is complex, and possibly capricious. They are likely to be of interest, owing to an ability to think outside of a lazy consensus. I doubt that such a person would have even the slimmest chance of working for the FCA. This is the essence of the problem.

Citywire covered the issues around the Section 166 review, and the concerns raised as part of this process. I was not associated with WealthTek in 2022, so I cannot offer any substantive comments. I can only note that it appears extraordinary that a review into the operations of the WealthTek business did not incorporate the concerns I had earlier raised. At the very least, it should have included a study of cash flows out of the business, and their connections with accounts associated with John. The Potemkin Village was still standing. Early March 2024, we learned that the FCA has gained permission to pause the civil case, with a 12 month stay to investigate criminal activity, incorporating fraud and money laundering. The two are of course interrelated, as when the proceeds derived from fraud are filtered into the broader economy, this is money laundering. Here, we meet the next problem.

It is the FCA who are investigating John and WealthTek. Furthermore, should the case go with trial, it will be The FCA v Jonathan (John as I knew him) Edward Dance and WealthTek. The civil proceedings, from outset, have certainly been structured in this manner. The problem being, it is not possible to investigate John, and WealthTek, without understanding the catastrophic failure of the FCA's anti-money laundering, authorisation, enforcement, and intelligence functions. They are two sides of the same coin, albeit, with likely differing motivations. If we are to assume that the fraud and money laundering happened, as alleged, and theorised by myself, it was a direct function of the failings of the FCA. In this regard, the FCA are partially conducting an investigation into their own failings. There is of course a but. The FCA do not want you to see it this way. Now, I take you back to my comments on the French Revoluation and time zero. As noted above, they are exceptionally well drilled, to the point of indoctrination, to deflect any narrative referring to events pre- April 2023. Some readers will be familiar with this tactic. Most recently, it was used extensively to deflect criticism over their failings relating to the scandals at London Capital & Finance, and Woodford Investment Management. Many concerns were raised about these businesses, well before the point of failure. The FCA use the time zero approach prolifically. Time that passes after time zero is very much their friend. Time before time zero is to the contrary, as it is accompanied by their old adversary, accountability. As soon as time zero is thrown down to anchor the narrative, they can immediately say that we cannot comment as there is an ongoing investigation. Even through, the investigation is a byproduct of their own failings. Then, if the case progresses to trial, they cannot comment, because there is an ongoing case. Time starts to look very accommodating. A complex trial is a very lengthy process. After this process passes, a long investigation may be launched. When it concludes, the world has often changed, with many other items hitting the news. People have moved on, and, quite tragically, some innocent victims may have passed. Time undergoes a metamorphosis from a potential adversary, into a friend. There is no real accountability, and the legal profession feasts on the misery of innocent victims. That is our society. We see it in so many forms. Be it the NHS, the police, or the Post Office. When institutions fail, they close ranks, which compounds the misery of those people they are charged to serve. It is sad indictment of modern society, particularly, here in the UK. When I asked the question, why are the FCA leading the investigation and legal process, I was met with puzzled and contemptuous looks. But it is a valid question. They lack the moral authority. They have failed to uphold the standards they demand of regulated firms, and individuals. If fraud and money laundering are proven beyond all reasonable doubt, or any indiscretions in the framework of the similarly unscientific balance of probabilities, it they who built the environment for it to happen. It is akin to a householder investigating a burglary, after neglecting to mention they left the front door wide open. The issue of legal impunity is also highly relevant. The FCA, under FSMA 2000, has inherited legal impunity. This is very controversial. Legal impunity was granted to prevent the regulator being frustrated in the course of fulfilling its statutory objectives. This is a privilege to be used responsibly. Sadly, it is all too often fulfilling the function of thwarting accountability. As the weeks passed, I was to discover that my frustrations with the FCA were shared.

Old Acquaintances

I was travelling on the Tyne & Wear Metro to Jesmond for a meeting when I received a message to call Tom Malloch. I had not spoken to Tom since I ended my association with Vertem Asset Management. Naturally, I understood the subject to be discussed, and called him as soon as I had a signal. It has been a very tough outcome for Malloch Melville, as the situation has destroyed their business, after years of hard work, and also had a ruinous impact on their clients. A terrible and undeserved reality for both. Tom was naturally upset, but still had the drive and energy to fight for clients of Malloch Melville. His professional income had ceased, following the special administration process. I explained about the unheeded warnings served to the FCA, commencing back in July 2021. Tom was shocked, and before attending my meeting, I sent him some of my exchanges with the FCA intelligence team. Tom was also in contact with his former colleague, Nigel Rawlins, and from the Vertem Asset Management side, Vinay Bedi. Soon we were exchanging our knowledge, and experiences, with the intention trying to help the WealthTek clients abandoned by the process. As I saw it, the FCA and HM Treasury, much to their collective disgrace, were operating a system of inverted morality. John was receiving what were termed reasonable expenses. In addition, consideration was given to the welfare of the horses subject to the then asset freeze, along with those who maintain them. This is understandable, as I am aware that there are innocent parties within the horse racing community, who are deserving of respect. Tragically, this is where is ended. The WealthTek clients, whose assets were frozen, were cynically abandoned, reinforced by the FCA's time zero tactic. What does this say about the morality of the UK? It is a deplorable window into the morality of officialdom. None of us were willing to accept this reality. We became an informal group, working for the dignity of the abandoned WealthTek clients. This is no mean undertaking and does come with risk. The FCA can be aggressive, and, on occasions, nefarious. Intoxicated by the unaccountability, facilitated by legal impunity, the FCA are not averse to making veiled threats over the careers of those who seek to hold them to account. Stretching back to my earlier career in Land Surveying, and contacts I had made working overseas, I have long engaged in collaborative research covering, amongst other things, corruption, and money laundering. My colleagues in this area were keen to provide me with some cover. Collectively, we started to conduct some detailed research into the FCA, and the methods they use. In the meantime, I also explained to the group how I had sought to warn Deborah Graham of

Ryecroft Glenton, and shared her response stating that all transactions were accounted for by John's drawings. Vinay put in considerable work in drafting a memorandum to be circulated to selected journalists, to highlight the inverted morality applied to the abandoned WealthTek clients, in the context of the dereliction of duty of the FCA. Vinay did a good job, and soon attracted the interest of Jonathan Ames of The Times. This presented me with a significant challenge. To gain traction, any story required me to be named, in a national newspaper, as the whistleblower, and to show several emails by way of substantiation. Up until that point, it was not widely known that I was the whistleblower, a term I dislike. I could have kept it this way but was aware of the distress the clients were experiencing. There were many very distressing accounts, which I found very troubling. The problem with whistleblowing in the current climate, is while there are many emails and calls expressing praise, ultimately, you are damaging your career. It was particularly tricky for me, as the FCA had failed to heed my warnings, much to the cost of WealthTek clients. This placed me in a vice-like position. Damage to my career, as it is inevitable that companies see whistleblowers as potential troublemakers, and an aggressive regulator, keen to shut down any notion of accountability. To put this situation into context, had I observed just a moderate level of contrition by the FCA, a mere face of humanity towards the suffering of the WealthTek clients, neither The Times article, nor this book, would have been published. It was an opportunity to shine a light on the self-serving institutional culture of the FCA, and the inverted morality directed towards WealthTek clients. I went ahead with it, with Nigel Rawlins also contributing. Jonathan Ames did a good job and had to cover a lot of ground. The article was published on 31st August 2023, and closely followed by an article by Citywire. In the days that followed, I spoke with Jack Gilbert, who covered the litany of FCA failures in a separate blogpost. The problem you encounter in these situations, is the attention span of the public can be short. They encounter a constant flow of news items. Something like the WealthTek situation will resonate for only a brief period of time. Many people will think to themselves, this is awful, I am glad that I am not in that situation. Then the next news item comes along, and the impact fades. It is like throwing a stone into a lake. There will be an initial impact. Then the stone silently descends to the deep. These outcomes serve failing institutions and politicians. The public must learn to exercise their collective human agency more effectively. Provided it is done in a nonviolent way, demonstrating displeasure at the ineptness at those paid so handsomely to serve us, does not make you a terrorist, nor an extremist. Things will not meaningfully change unless collectively, people stand up and make it clear that it is unacceptable. Similarly, do not let the established media peddle the line that all alternative platforms are centres for misinformation. Yes, they also need to be accountable, but established media can also be powerful sources of misinformation, not to mention, vehicles for censorship.

Taking a brief step back, a few weeks prior to the publication of The Times and Citywire articles, Tom Malloch, in his efforts to secure some dignity for his clients, had been in regular contact with Matthew Stone of BDO. He passed on my details to Stone, who made contact, proposing a meeting. I thought it could be beneficial to WealthTek clients, so I agreed. I do not doubt that BDO have had a tough task given the suggested duration of the shortfalls run by John's businesses. Nevertheless, I surprised, and disappointed, about how little Matthew knew about the structure of the business. I formed the impression that a lot of time had been wasted. It is easy to waste time when you are paid so handsomely for it. In the inverted mortality of this case, the WealthTek clients, the most innocent, are forced to pay the bill to assess the misuse of their own assets. Just pause at this point and ponder the morality of this situation. What does it tell you about the UK? Again, we meet the reality that in situations of self-serving institutional failure, the innocent suffers the most. The virtual meeting reminded me of my time running tutorials at Newcastle Business School. I had to completely reshape their thinking, explaining the evolution of the John's businesses, in the manner covered above. The three distinct phases, and how I had developed my theory. This was mid-August 2023, and BDO had commenced their work in April of the same year. The standard of questions asked did not convey the impression of substantive progress. Matthew Stone could dispute this; he is entitled to his own opinion. However, if we were to review the conversation, it would not, I feel, do him considerable credit. He was polite, and keen to listen, but I was disappointed for the WealthTek clients. Yes, the reconciliation of client assets is all important. What I could not understand is the accompanying approach. I would have immediately asked for a past, and present, staff list, commencing by endeavouring to make contact with the most experienced staff to leave the organisation. This would have provided early, and valuable, intelligence to assist the reconciliation, and the historic shortfalls. This strikes at the heart of the problem. There is a fundamental misalignment between the interests of the Special Administrator, and the WealthTek clients. It is very easy to order expensive, and pleasant food, when somebody else is footing the bill. I was contacted by a client of WealthTek. He has been greatly impacted by this situation. He was a loyal, and early client of Vertem Asset Management. He too was frustrated by the audit process, and the lack of alignment of interests. He explained that BDO told him I was only a consultant, with limited knowledge. It is ironic that I was the first person to identify the risks of fraud, some two years earlier. The selection process of the Special Administrator is far too opaque. It was stated that the FCA approached BDO about the role at the end of March 2023. How competitive was this process? Beyond this, of the vast legal counsel costs incurred by BDO during the special administration process, how were the legal professionals chosen and costed? The process has treated many of the WealthTek clients with contempt, particularly the longest serving. I will return to this point later in the book. Swinging back to The Times and Citywire articles, as we moved into September 2023, I received another polite email from Matthew Stone.

In observing data protection protocol, Stone notified me that the FCA had been in touch asking for my contact details. Correctly, he asked for my permission to provide such. I consented. The FCA were ponderously stirring into action. Belatedly, they had realised that the Potemkin Village they had so keenly endorsed, had a good deal more occurring behind the panels. I received an email from the lead investigator, copying in her team, including the manager who was to assume operational control. By this time, my research colleagues and I had undertaken considerable research into FCA methods, including investigations. I had mixed emotions. Based on my meeting with Stone, I deduced that their investigation was unlikely to be in a healthy state. I replied by raising the issue of the Chambers speech, and also asked why it had taken The Times article to stir them into action, as the clients of WealthTek were suffering? The response I received was extraordinary. She stated that I had been identified as a person of interest, and The Times article had expediated the matter. Identifying me as a person of interest would have amounted to ten seconds of work, via a visit to the Companies House site. But it got even more bizarre. She claimed that the intelligence unit had not informed the investigation operation that I was the whistleblower. This was absolutely extraordinary. This typifies the issue. This was in September. A major theme of this book is FCA failures created the environment for John, if my theory, and their allegations are correct, to misuse client assets, and launder money. I again pressed on the Chambers speech, and she remembered her time zero training. As I hope readers now appreciate, time zero is the FCA's mitigation strategy to deflect the reality that their failures, and the allegations standing against John, are two side of the same coin. At this point, she became more aggressive, and quoted the powers of investigators under FSMA 2000 and so on. I remind her that the FCA had grossly failed to meet its own statutory, and operational objectives. There was a little more swashbuckling over the details of the interview, and she became more conciliatory, which allowed us to move forward. I was happy to help them in the context of intelligence, as I could see that they were in a real mess. However, I was not going to be bullied by a regulator that had failed clients and instituted a system of inverted morality. I invited the FCA to Do the right thing. What I came to realise is whenever I reminded them that their failures had contributed to real human suffering, it was as if my words disappeared into a vortex. They had been trained, as is common across a good many of institutions in the UK, to ignore inconvenient questions. I can categorically state, that at no point in my interactions with the FCA, have I ever felt that this case is about the clients of WealthTek. It has always felt that this case is about cleaning up their own reputation. The client outcome being a byproduct of their primary objective. This is why this book has been written. After some further interactions, we agreed a date for my compelled interview. Tom Malloch had also received his calling. It was clear that their expediated investigation had gone little further than being shaken out by The Time article, and canvassing BDO for other names. It had the appearance of a very clumsy affair.

Napoleon and Josphine

The FCA like to conduct compelled interviews in pairs. In my case, the Lead Investigator, and her colleague. In the days leading to the agreed date, I received my interview bundle. I was off to the home of Napoleon and Joshine, at least in name. I have to respect the FCA's investigation, so I cannot cover the bundle, only to note that it told me a good deal where they were in the process. Not very far, considering we were in mid-October 2023. Due diligence had also been conducted on both interviewers, so I had an idea what to expect. I knew the team were staying in the hotel, so with a 10am start scheduled, I arranged to meet a friend for breakfast at 8:30am. It seemed a reasonable guess for their breakfast time. The team had chosen a corner table, which gave me good visibility. You can lean a good deal in observing the behaviour, and interactions of people, even from a distance, at a breakfast table. I could gauge their temperament, and how they work together. After breakfast, I left for a walk, and pondered what I had seen. They were reasonable and benign. Before finding them, there were a few other things I needed to verify in the context of the activities of the team. I then asked the hotel receptionist where I could find them, and so we began. The interview letter had given no instructions about how we were to meet. There is a lot of protocol to go through, and then the questions commenced. They ask questions in blocks, so the recording can be transcribed in bite sized blocks for the typists. Part of our research in the methods deployed by the FCA, had placed me on alert with regards recording and transcripts, so I took precautions. I had done the same with BDO.

I observed them closely when giving my answers, as I could gauge when I was providing them with information that was fresh, and what they already knew. I felt that they were struggling. I estimated that the bundle, which comprised one exhibit again confirming that they did not look behind the panels of the Potemkin Village, and data which I assume was sourced from BDO, was no more than ten minutes work. They were only particular familiar with the data. I found the questions boring, and so tried to take the initiative and help them. Like BDO, they had little understanding of the business, and how it had evolved. I felt like I had to change their way of thinking, otherwise they would get nowhere fast. They were polite, but the whole occasion came to again remind me of running at seminar at Newcastle Business School. I did genuinely try to help them as best I could, and also emailed them when fresh thoughts, or information, came my way. I did, however, find it very difficult to trust the FCA. This was a reflection of the lack of humility on their part. I believe that there is a cultural issue at the FCA. An arrogant air of unaccountability.

Before the interview, I made it clear to the FCA that I would play no part in any legal process. In this regard, I will use my human agency, and will not succumb to bullying, and coercion. I also made it clear that the information that I provided, was for the purpose of intelligence to assist their investigation and must not be used in the legal process. On the latter, the person claiming to have operational control of the investigation, who has since been content with his name appearing in the media, disputed, citing FSMA 2000. I will summarise why I do not consent. First, I will not support any process which operates under a system of inverted morality, where the most innocent people are left abandoned. Second, the FCA has failed meet its regulatory and operational objectives set out in FSMA 2000. Therefore, I consider the arguments used under FSMA 2000 to be void. Third, the FCA has failed to hold itself to the same standards demanded of those it regulates. Fourth, FCA failures cannot be considered separately from the alleged misconduct of John, they are two sides of the same coin. I reject the time zero approach, as I believe it is motivated by a desire to frustrate any accountability. In summary, I do not believe that the FCA has the moral authority, or integrity, to bring the case. I have not been able to satisfy myself that their motivations are primarily driven by protecting the consumers they failed so badly. There have been catastrophic failures in the FCA's anti-money laundering, authorisation, enforcement, and intelligence functions. The noted failings have gravely undermined the whistleblowing function, which adds additional risk to the financial system. Potential whistleblowers will no doubt consider this case and come to the conclusion that it is not worth the risk to their careers. I hold a further concern, which I have raised with the FCA. I believe they have an inclination to try to right a wrong, with a wrong. In this respect, I cannot be confident by what I have seen thus far, that John would receive a fair trial, should he be charged. This must not be confused with a desire to justify any of the alleged wrongdoing. I will return to these points later in the book.

Finally, on the recorded interview and transcript, the FCA, when prompted, sought to make these available via egress. I do not personally trust egress as encrypted portal, and at no time did the FCA have my informed consent for it to be used as a method of transfer. I rejected their argument that they, and many other institutions, prolifically use egress as a method of transfer. I do not accept that the extensive use of a service, is necessarily an endorsement. It merely means that you are copying the action of others, and intend on using this as an excuse, when shortcomings arise. I believe that my concerns over egress will, in time, be justified. I actually only desired a copy of the typed transcript. I did, after some weeks receive a USB stick, with an emailed password. Naturally, it is very high risk to insert a third-party device into a computer, so I enlisted the services of a research associate, who is an expert in this field. The device was scanned and deemed to be unsafe. I have since given up hope of receiving a typed transcript. It is therefore important to note, that I cannot be certain that the information provided, has been used with an appropriate degree of integrity.

Challenging Inverted Morality

During, and after, the respective compelled interviews, I continued to work with my former associates to challenge the inverted mortality instituted by the FCA. Tom Malloch, Nigel Rawlings, Vinay Bedi, and Adrian Buck, all worked hard to help abandoned WealthTek clients. Clients awaiting their fate, as the BDO reconciliation rolled on, and costs mounted. Of particular concern, were the obscene legal counsel costs. Clients continued to be without access to their investments. The stories of distress were increasing. Individual tragedies. John continued to have access to reasonable living expenses. In addition, clients have to pick up the costs of the special administration process. The most innocent suffer the most. The system of inverted morality. An unacceptable reality, given the two sides of the same coin of FCA failure, and John's alleged misconduct. A reality frustrated by the time zero approach. Another distasteful aspect was the opacity of the Creditors Committee. This created a two-tier system of information, and treated the clients not connected to members of the committee, with the upmost contempt. Many clients were reliant on word of mouth, or had to check the Stellar Asset Management website, in the hope of a few scraps of information, as the guidance for the receipt of their statements continued to slide. For an economy with pretensions of hosting a world class financial services sector, this was a disgraceful situation. Even though I had ended my association with Vertem Asset Management over two years prior, I did not feel comfortable leaving clients of WealthTek abandoned. Furthermore, although I did not have a direct relationship with the clients of Vertem Asset Management, I was always very grateful to them, and feel distraught about the situation they face.

Tom Malloch, and Nigel Rawlings, have made contact with their respective MPs, with the hope of vanquishing the monstrous inverted morality. I have tried to reason with the FCA, but they remain well drilled in their inhuman time zero approach. Collectively, we just want a gesture. In my thoughts, BDO's fees should be met by The Treasury. In addition, I am concerned that the assets held under the now Restraint Order, are at risk of significant impairment. As with the costs of the special administration process, the impairment risk of the assets subject to the Restraint Order, fall on the clients, should a criminal conviction be secured. I do, however, acknowledge that the FCA have placed WealthTek clients in a potentially better position, with Restraint Order, which is wider in scope than the Worldwide Freezing Order. Tom and Nigel have followed correct protocol by seeking to work with their respective MPs. The hope is they can lobby the Treasury Committee, to acknowledge the failings of the FCA, and make a belated gesture to provide some relief to the neglected, innocent clients of WealthTek. One of the MPs contacted, Keir Mather, was a sitting member of the committee at the time. I commended their efforts. I did, however, find myself in a more cynical mindset, whilst hoping to be proven wrong. I see politicians as very much part of the problem. Slippery creatures, who merely use their constituents as conduits for their own betterment. They exemplify the concept of forgetting who serves whom. In addition, other than hollow political posturing, I cannot recall the Treasury Committee ever doing anything worthwhile. Nigel Rawlins had a very worthwhile idea. He has looked into the fines that the FCA have imposed on errant business, which appear to be harvested by HM Treasury, and made the suggestion to his MP that a small proportion of this yield could go a long way, should it be allocated to paying the special administration fee, in the context of the devasting failures of the FCA. This is an eminently sensible, and just suggestion. I understand that the suggestion what not favoured by Economic Secretary to the Treasury, Bim Afolami. I would duly invite Afolami to take a moment to reflect if he is morally fit for public office. I will return to Afolami later in the book. At this juncture, I would also invite reader to reflect. Should it ever have been necessary for either of us to press so hard for what are basic acts of humanity? Sadly, this was very much necessary. I wonder, what does this say about the self-serving elites that run our society? I often look no further to Andrew Bailey, Governor of the Bank of England. Bailey was a disaster during his time with the FCA and was rewarded with the top job at the Bank of England. I then recall Bailey trying to convince us that the post Covid-19 related inflation, was merely transitory. Even laypersons knew this to be nonsense. Let us not forget him seemingly being unaware of the embedded risks within the Liability Driven

Investment (LDI) strategies, used within the pensions market, which were alarmingly exposed following the disastrous mini budget delivered under the short-lived Prime Ministership of Liz Truss. Look at David Cameron. Cameron resigned as leader of The Conservative Party, following calling, and misjudging, a referendum on the UK's membership of the European Union. This followed his much hyped, but tragically unsuccessful, attempt to win concessions for the UK on migration ahead of the historic vote. This being the height of his foreign policy endeavours, we then find him shoehorned into the Foreign Secretary role, and to make matters worse, following some political gratuities, he is not even directly accountable to the House of Commons. It is important to understand that these matters do not stand in isolation to the concerns raised in this book. Unaccountable, self-serving elites.

As the sliding guidance for clients to receive their statements, eventually threatened to become a reality, we all greatly dreaded the moment for WealthTek clients. You might say, that other than feeling greatly concerned for their welfare, I did not have skin in the game. I did not ever have a direct client relationship with the clients of Vertem Asset Management, nor have I ever used this exhausting process as a way to pitch for business. However, not only is standing up for the most innocent in this distressing affair a just cause, but it also has wider implications. If institutional failure is consistently buried, we will see more outcomes like The Post Office, and WealthTek. None of us are immune to institutional failure, and indifference. In the case of the FCA, this regulator has a disgraceful track record of failing those they are charged with protecting, and then abandoning them to insincerities of time. It is very easy to assume that this could never happen to you. It could. The way to stop it is standing by those who have been let down and holding failing institutions to account. When the statements started to become available to the clients of WealthTek, it was like a drip feed of distressing news. It would be inappropriate to name clients, but I became aware of the circumstances faced by very loyal clients of Vertem Asset Management, hardworking, good, honest people. Many are now elderly, and into the retirement phases of their lives. Those with SIPPs face additional difficulties, as the Financial Services Compensation Scheme (FSCS) payments fall outside of their pension. Furthermore, the FSCS payments, are up to a maximum of £85,000, the real value of which has been eroded by many years of inflation, are subject to adjustments to reflect that the WealthTek clients are obliged to pay for the special administration, despite being innocent parties, and oblivious to the gross failings of the FCA. What became apparent is the longest serving clients, those connected to Vertem Asset Management and Malloch Melville, and, especially those with liquid holdings, such as collective investment schemes, and widely held direct equities, were hit hardest. From what I could deduced from the limited cases I had been made aware of, suggested that funds had been raised in an arbitrary fashion. I need this sum, so what is the most efficient, and discreet way of raising it. If a portfolio fitted this profile, unfortunately, the client got disproportionately hit. It looked like a sweep for liquidity. In some ways it reminded me of examples where ruthless dictators had raided the national wealth of their countries, and spent it on lavish lifestyles, uncaring of the suffering of the general populace. There was a callous indifference about the outcome. Again, writing in the context of no charges having been raised, I could not help noticing that even people well known to John, had been severely impacted. I thought back to the Mike Bains situation, it must take a callous mindset to sit in front of people, knowing their hopes, their dreams, their struggles, to then engage in devastatingly destructive actions. Can the pull of mammon, materialism, and the cult of the microcelebrity, be so strong? Perhaps it can. But the force multiplier from the perspective of the most innocent, is the institutional self-interest of the FCA, and HM Treasury. I feel that there has been a misconception in this situation. It is very easy for the general public to dismiss the relevance of WealthTek, on the grounds of it being a mere example of one rich person, availing themselves of the property of others of the same category. In the vast majority of cases, nothing could be further from this perception. In addition, for those exceptions, this does not justify the loss, and terrible breach of trust. Vinay Bedi did a very good job of addressing these misconceptions, when participating in Nick Luck podcast. He focused on the human cost the WealthTek situation. There were a few misconceptions about the Restraint Order. It is not as simple as just crystallising value in horses and other assets. It is my understanding that John cannot be forced to sell assets. The value can only be salvaged after a criminal conviction, and a subsequent confiscation order. Neither Vinay, Nigel, nor I, crave media attention. The inverted morality of the case pushed us into it.

Naturally, much of the focus of this book has been on the WealthTek clients, but I have also used the broader term, stakeholders. I cannot do justice to all those impacted, as a result of what has happened at WealthTek. I will, however, focus on Malloch Melville. I noted earlier in the book that it is not my place to tell the story of this business. Tom Malloch does require some coverage. He has been badly impacted. To understand the extent of this, requires familiarisation with another misconception. From outset, Malloch Melville has been named as a trading name of WealthTek, in a similar fashion to Vertem Asset Management. Whilst this is true, the two are also very different. The way it has been presented in the media, and to a large extent by the FCA, is that both businesses were controlled by John. This is not true. Vertem Asset Management was owned and controlled by John. Whereas Malloch Melville, was in essence a service user. They utilised the infrastructure, and regulatory permissions, of

WealthTek. From Tom's perspective, he and his colleagues were working hard to build up, and grow, their own asset management business. Despite all the setbacks that John created for them, they had reached a viable level. The future was looking promising. As I acknowledged earlier in the book, there were occasions during my association with Vertem Asset Management, where I envied Malloch Melville, as they were on the same journey we had originally embarked upon. Tom and his colleagues did not have any operational control, or influence, at WealthTek. Imagine working exceptionally hard to establish your own business, and then suddenly it is frozen. Then, you discover that a sizable proportion of your clients' assets have disappeared. Sadly, it gets worse. Then imagine that the special administrators, and the FCA, recommend that what is left is allocated to other businesses. Who would not feel heartbroken and aggrieved at this outcome? There will be many other tragedies that have resulted from the WealthTek situation, spanning multiple other sectors, not only financial services. I am sorry that I have not been able to convey all of them. Actions have extended consequences. There is no one definitive story, only many separate tragedies.

Before moving on, the WealthTek situation has not been without bouts of sanctimony. One example of such, would be the position taken by Stellar Asset Management, after the reconciliation of client assets by the special administrator, BDO. I am of course pleased that their clients experienced only minor losses, in respect to the failure of WealthTek, which will largely be addressed by the FSCS payments. However, whatever the narrative this business pursues regarding systems that were in place to protect the assets of their clients, one thing that is certain, their due diligence process in selecting WealthTek as a platform, was an absolute disaster. Even the most elementary of research would have identified serious concerns. This includes John's lifestyle, visits to Companies House, and questioning the business case for a platform that could never hope to compete against much better capitalised peers. It was somewhat ironic that they refer to the success of their investment process, in the context of not being able to recognise the warnings signs from a curious glance at John LLPs, let alone his regulatory permissions. The compliance function of their business, which should have been embedded in the process for the selection of a platform, failed badly.

Tweedledum and Tweedledee

I can understand the desire of the FCA to pursue the WealthTek case through the criminal justice system. But I cannot state that I believe this desire is primarily motivated by the welfare of WealthTek clients. It has always been my impression, that the interest of WealthTek clients, were usurped by preserving the reputation of the FCA, and, by extension, the UK financial services sector. As I have noted consistently, the alleged misconduct of John, and the failings of the FCA, are two sides of the same coin. They are, in many respects, indistinguishable. Tweedledum and Tweedledee. The application for a 12 month stay of the civil case, to allow the FCA to focus on building a criminal case, in many respects, makes sense. To run both cases together, would be costly, and time consuming. The Judge made the order, and so they got their wish. However, there were some troubling aspects. These concerns are in the theme of those featured throughout this book. Based on information that has been made public, I will review these aspects.

I will start with the allegation that John falsified his regulatory permissions, by forging an authorisation document, issued by the FCA, stating the scope of permission for the then Vertus Asset Management LLP, in January 2020. The permissions did not include safeguarding and administering assets, which were, allegedly, added, via a forgery of the original document. WealthTek then went on to deny holding client money, or assets, and concealed these functions. During the process, John agreed withdraw the application to hold these permissions. As the shortfall in assets significantly pre-dated this application, and extended back to 2014, during the Sapia relationship, this would have put John in a very difficult situation. Had he transferred to another platform, which held these permissions, this would have entailed a full audit. One would imagine such an exercise would have identified the shortfall. This chimes with my theory on the WealthTek platform. The platform, which I never believed made sense in such a competitive environment, was built for the purposes of concealing the existing shortfalls, and possibly perpetrating further such actions. Therefore, in the context agreeing to withdraw the application to safeguard and administer client assets, John would have been faced with either giving himself up, or forging the document outlining the scope of permission, to conceal, and perpetrate, the fraud. This also takes us back to the Potemkin Village, approved by the FCA. The FCA approved John for performing the significant management function, and compliance oversight. The FCA, by not looking behind the panels of the Potemkin Village, overlook the reality that there was no independent compliance oversight. This is exceptionally dangerous and demonstrates a significant weakness in the

FCA's regulatory architecture. The FCA allowed themselves to become Potemkin Village idiots. According to the allegations made by the FCA, John was then able to use the forged document, to mislead other institutions, such as Barclays Bank, CACEIS and, in a different context, Novia Financial. The latter being used as part of a subterfuge to mislead the FCA. Presumably, Barclays Bank and CACEIS, could have checked the FCA register at any time, but merely relied on a forged letter. This is hardly a ringing endorsement for the sophistication, and integrity of the UK's financial services sector, which claims to be world-class. It more resembles a frontier market debacle.

Then we have the allegations of money laundering. This personal use of the proceeds fraud. There are a few points to note here. Again, we must return to the FCA's approval of the Potemkin Village. In addition to waving through no independent compliance oversight, the FCA approved a person without the requisite experience for the role. What I have metaphorically termed, falling to check behind the panels. I ended my association with Vertem Asset Management in May 2021, so I saw little of the WealthTek operation, especially given the long period of homeworking. However, the impression I formed, is John recruited more experienced operational staff after my time. But he still had a notable intellectual advantage over them, only less so than in the chaotic Sapia period. The FCA were not the only Potemkin Village idiots. Those working in operations, compliance, and portfolio management present themselves as experienced, and qualified professionals, on LinkedIn, but, if the allegations are correct, they could not spot a fraud, and money laundering, happening right under their noises. I do wonder what this tells us about industry standards of education. What good are professional qualifications if you cannot see a fraud happening before your eyes? It has been quite telling looking at the rhetorical back peddling that has occurred. I return to James Flintoft. AJ Bell put out press releases notifying that James Flintoft had joined them at the start of February 2023. The notices stated that James was Head of Portfolio Management at Vertem Asset Management and had managed a Model Portfolio Service. The latter in singular form was not strictly true and had ceased nearly two years prior to the announcement. Then, after the special administration of WealthTek, James seemingly worked for a regional discretionary fund manager. Either he worked for Vertem Asset Management, running the portfolio management function, or he did not? It cannot be both, and why the need for camouflage? We also have prominent financial UK financial institutions, which do not have systems in place to spot copious suspicious transactions. Instead, they cling hold to a forged letter, with an extra permission, or two, added. This, we are invited to believe is the robustness of the FCA's anti-money laundering regime. The UK has an embarrassing record in the field of money laundering. It has long been one of the key global centres for financial crime. One of the problems being, although money laundering has technical definitions, its interpretation is often political. When it suited the UK, Russian money flowed freely through the financial system, the real estate market, independent schools, and, of course, the Premier League. Naturally, politicians, officials, and legal professionals, also enjoyed their share. But when the politics changes, it is suddenly money laundering. Even though, nothing else changes. The source of money was unchanged. My guess is we will, at some point, see the same process with Saudi money. There will come a time when the Saudi's decline to do what the UK and US wishes, and then, all of a sudden, they will be money launders. It is just not credible. The FCA pushes institutions to harass ordinary people, who are engaging in straightforward transactions, and misses, or perhaps in a geopolitical sense, chooses to miss, high level examples. In this example, a mere forged letter did the trick. Nothing more sophisticated that a school kid forging a parent's letter to swerve swimming lessons. The FCA is keen to present itself as a leader in FinTech, and cryptocurrency regulation. This is absolutely absurd. What use are regulatory sandboxes, if a cut and paste letter is all it takes to navigate the system?

Matters get even more farcical, as the FCA have realised that John concealed a bankruptcy from them, during the course of the WealthTek application for direct authorisation. The bankruptcy order was made in July 2018, with HMRC as the creditor. What this suggests, is it would have been more difficult for John to secure credit to purchase a sofa, than to be approved for senior management functions, and compliance oversight, at a financial services business. A financial services sector which claims to be world class. The Potemkin Village, and the Potemkin Village idiots. He even used some chicanery with his name. Variants being Jonathan and Johnathan. Incidentally, I have used John throughout this book, as that is the name he preferred me to use. When I look at the information that is accessible to the public, I do wonder if the FCA actually know who they are trying to prosecute? At this point, I invite readers to consider the Jabez Spencer Balfour example. A financial villain of the late Victorian era. Apart from the FCSC, is the current regulatory architecture overseen by the FCA really any better? Investors need to be vigilant when operating at levels over the maximum payout of £85,000. Particularly, given the terrible shortcomings of the FCA, who will cut you adrift should a default, or failure, occur. You will even have to pick up the bill to assess the damage. Inverted morality, reinforced by the time zero approach, and legal impunity. The alleged wrongdoings, and the FCA's failings, are indeed Tweedledum and Tweedledee. In summary, your protections predominantly rest with the honesty of your investment professional, which, in the great majority of cases, will be fine. The FCA is merely your Fairweather friend.

The discovery of further alleged misconduct between 2014 and 2020, during the Sapia period, does at least suggest that they, somewhat belatedly, listened to my theory. As noted earlier, this I related to both BDO, and the FCA, in the months of August 2023 and October 2023, respectively. This they might try to dispute, but records will prove otherwise. In addition, neither mentioned earlier shortfalls, until after these dates. It also takes us back to the earlier points I made about the dangers of distance compliance relationships, where one company uses the regulatory permissions of another. This does not mean that such instances will indicate fraud. However, such arrangements should be considered higher risk, from the prospective of a client. As noted throughout the book, I found the manner in which the Sapia relationship came to an end confusing. However, I was not privy to the discussion, as my role was purely investment research. There were compliance visits, and audits were undertaken, but, if the allegations are true, the level of supervisions must have been inadequate. These types of arrangements will need an urgent review, to ensure client assets are safe in the context of any supervisions vacuums that may exist. As I write this book, financial markets were amid an artificial intelligence boom. I wonder if more focus should be placed on our intelligence. Running a financial services business is not easy. If a person running a financial services business is engaging in extensive activities in other sectors, with explosive displays of opulence, surely this should warrant some attention? Does this business have appropriate checks and balances in place? In the case of Vertem Asset Management, under the Sapia relationships, or as a directly authorised WealthTek, these displays were far from hidden. They were part of a narcissistic push for microcelebrity status. Starting with our early media coverage at Vertem Asset Management, leading to focus on horse racing, a clear pattern could have been deduced. This evolution was not itself a definitive sign that client assets were being misused. But it clearly warranted attention, and much closer scrutiny.

I will now traverse back to the earlier concerns raised over the fairness of the legal process. This links closely to concerns that I have raised with the FCA, over potentially trying to right a wrong, with a wrong. Naturally, I believe that if John is found to be guilty of misusing client assets, and money laundering, he must be punished. But the process must be fair and transparent. The FCA, whose failings are of course a fundamental part of this situation, have drawn attention to John not answering the allegations against him. They have been less vocal about their own inability to apologise to WealthTek clients for catastrophic failures, and the delivery of the Chambers speech, which gave a false and misleading impression of expediency. There is one aspect which is particularly troubling. When John was arrested in April 2023, his laptop was seized, and since this time, he was not had access to his emails, or any other data stored on the WealthTek servers. In this regard, the FCA and their legal representatives have been able to cherry pick evidence to use in court process. This allows them to dictate proceedings, and the context with which evidence is presented. This is not worthy of a legal process in a civilised society. Furthermore, I am concerned that this represents a violation of his human rights, under Article 6 of the European Convention on Human Rights. If he is to prepare a defence, there should be no asymmetries of evidence. John, and his legal representatives, should have equal access to this information. If the case against John is so strong, why deny access to this information? What is there to hide? There needs to be a through, and transparent, audit to discount the risk of the concealment and falsification of evidence. I am particularly concerned about this risk in the context of the much-discussed time zero approach of the FCA. Shutting down and suppressing avenues of accountability, despite being tainted by the disgrace of incompetence, and misleading the public. I could, of course be mistaken, but for the interest of integrity, this risk must be discounted. If such practice were to occur in China, Iran, or Russia, I would imagine the UK would be a very vocal critic, if there were geopolitical opportunities in doing so. The FCA, and their methods, along with the structure of legal proceedings, have caused concerns, even within the European Union. In this regard, the case of Global plc, and the FCA's pursuit of Konstantinos Papadimitraopoulos and Dimitris Gryparis for the criminal offences of fraud and making misleading statements about the value of Globo's shares, prior to the demise of the business in November 2015, appears relevant. In February 2019, the FCA obtained domestic and European Arrest Warrants, for both the aforementioned named. The warrants were denied by the Hellenic Court of Appeal, whereupon the Greek authorities instituted their own criminal proceedings, which, as the FCA acknowledged, were substantially similar to those they were themselves intending to prosecute. Both were acquitted. Now, as with John, I make no claims of innocence. In the Globo case, the issues boiled down to methods used in the procurement of evidence, and concerns over a fair trial. Here rest my concerns. It is the FCA, and the methods they use, which is the problem. This is why I cannot have any personal involvement in this case. There were too many shortcomings of integrity and morality. The incompetency, along with the lack of integrity, and morality of the FCA, created the architectural backdrop for the Potemkin Village, and the ensuing suffering of WealthTek clients. Sadly, the UK has an unfortunate relationship with the European Convention of Human Rights. We need look at only the treatment of Jullian Assange. Only his sheer will, and determination to live, has kept him alive. It could be interpreted that both the UK, and US, are seeking to murder him by attrition, for the crime of exposing the truth, and seeking public accountability. Seeking to do this is becoming ever more perilous in the UK. A country that believes it is humane, and indeed cost effective, to process asylum applications in Rwanda. The same country that believes it is humane to imprison asylum seekers on boats. If a country imprisons people for exposing the truth, then it really is not such a big step. The UK is taking a very dangerous path, and has unfortunately, voluntarily, surrendered its moral authority to hold to account other countries in the area of human rights. I return to my earlier point over the fitness of the FCA to bring this case. I firmly maintain that the catastrophic incompetence, and desire to mislead the public with the time zero approach, best typified by the Chambers statement, makes them morally unsuitable to bring this case. They simply do not have the integrity to do so. They have a role to play as the regulator, but I believe the case should have been led by the Serious Fraud Office, who, in the context of this case, are not obviously encumbered by the disgrace of mass incompetence. The FCA should play a supportive role only. The Serious Fraud Office, in a similar fashion to the FCA, can operate as the investigative and prosecuting authority. It is quite ironic that the investigator claiming to have operational control of the case, a person who has since been content to name himself in public, despite the making great noise about the lack of defence offered by John, has himself exhibited stunning incompetence. As late as January 2024, this individual still did not know the extent of my association with Vertem Asset Management. In an email, he described me as an employee/partner of WealthTek. I was of course neither. Despite walking the FCA through the evolution and structure of the business in very gentle steps during my interview, I am not confident that they have a firm understanding of what they are investigating. In suggesting this case could be the largest individual fraud by an approved person, the same person neglects to mention, perhaps this is also the FCA's biggest failure. The coin they do not want to turn.

Returning back to why the FCA is pursuing this case, despite appearing to not possess the moral authority, or integrity to do so, it will be necessary to consider some interesting aspects. The Judge, when considering the legal framework for justifying The Stay, noted, as I have done so above, the unique position of the FCA as regulator, criminal investigator and, ultimately, prosecutor. But, from this point, it starts to get rather interesting. The Judge went on to note that this is reinforced by Parliament's clear imposition on the FCA, of the statutory operational objectives, which includes protecting, and enhancing the integrity of the UK's financial system. Well, well, well. This is very interesting indeed, as we already know that the FCA has catastrophically failed in these objectives, and also issued false and misleading statements to the public in the process. What we are starting to see here, is the UK's legal and financial systems are far from the envy of the world. Let us start with the regulatory objectives under FSMA 2000, which, in broad terms, fall under the following headings:

Market confidence

Financial stability

Public awareness

The protection of consumers

The reductions of financial crime

I would hope that readers can determine from the narrative that there have been catastrophic failures in four of the five areas. The WealthTek situation is not large enough to have caused instability in the system. The fourth and fifth categories, noted above, need no further explanation, as they are clear catastrophic failures by the FCA. In the instance that readers may query market confidence and public awareness, I will deal with each in turn. Starting with market confidence, we know that by signing off the Potemkin Village, the FCA has devasted market confidence. Minus the FCSC, the FCA have taken us back to the time of Jabez Spencer Balfour. They have also destroyed the integrity of the whistleblowing function. In this area, they have tried to cover their backs, in fearing a backlash from the WealthTek scandal. One notable example being the news item posted by the FCA on 27th February 2024, FCA to improve the pace and transparency of enforcement cases. The FCA have also issued a various pieces covering whistleblowing. All of these lack substance. They are combinations of words without meaning. There are little incentives for whistleblowers to risk their careers, when they are met with a useless intelligence team, who do not understand the significance of the information provided. Let us now move to public awareness. There is a clear failure on public awareness, as the Chambers statement provided a false and misleading impression to the public of the expediency of FCA action over WealthTek. Chambers has made no attempts to apologise, which represents a disgraceful lack of professionalism. An early client of Vertem Asset Management wrote to both Chambers and Rathi, complaining about the inappropriate tone of the speech, amongst other things, back in September 2023, and as of April 2024, had not received even an acknowledgement. What hope is there for a market, when senior officials at the regulator behave in such as disrespectful manner. I would encourage both to reflect on their fitness and propriety to fulfil their current roles.

Let us now look at the operational objectives of the FCA, which were mentioned in the context of the case. These are as follows:

Protect consumers from bad conduct.

Protect the integrity of the financial system.

Promote effective competition in the interests of consumers.

The first two are clear catastrophic failures. The third is more open to interpretation, and in many ways, rests beyond the scope of this book. As noted above, I have always regarded the FCA, as a regulator for its own convenience. After their catastrophic failures over WealthTek, there is a risk that the FCA will make it very difficult for smaller wealth, and asset management businesses, to compete. I believe they may lean towards a fewer number of giant businesses that they can periodically waive a stick at. Consumer Duty certainly has undertones of this in its application so far. A relentless focus on cost to drive consolidation. Whilst I believe that the application for The Stay was not unreasonable, the legal framework to justify it, was based on an act of parliament, against which the FCA has catastrophically failed. This leads me to the secondary objective, which is most interesting in the context of the WealthTek case, and the indifference of the FCA, and HM Treasury, to the suffering of clients. The secondary objective is defined accordingly:

Facilitating, subject to aligning with relevant international standards:

The international competitiveness of the UK (including in particular the financial services sector), and its growth in the medium to long-term.

The FCA's catastrophic failures in the Wealth Tek case, has exposed the UK financial services sector as having vulnerabilities that are below what might be expected in a frontier market. As we have seen, the FCA approved the Potemkin Village, and failed to look behind the panels. If the allegations are proven, it would have been more challenging for John to obtain credit to purchase a modestly priced sofa, than it was for him to secure senior management, and compliance oversight permissions. In addition, all it took was cutting and pasting on extra permissions to a letter, to then proceed to commit fraud, and launder tens of millions of pounds. This is all it took to fool a regulator, and a number of supposedly sophisticated financial services businesses, you cannot claim to promote the competitiveness of a market, if its controls are below what might be expected of frontier equivalent. I therefore contend, the welfare of the WealthTek clients, has been sacrificed on the altar of the FCA's secondary objective. This is why they have deployed the time zero approach. This is why they cut WealthTek clients adrift. It could thus be argued that the legal proceedings are predominantly motivated by defending this objective, not fighting for the welfare of the WealthTek client they failed so badly. This could equally be why HM Treasury has been similarly indifferent. The UK's financial services sector was in decline even before Brexit. London's role as a financial centre is simply no longer as relevant as in the past. With integrated European financial markets, London's role is far diminished. Why would a large global business choose London for a listing? It does not make sense. The integrated European markets of Amsterdam, Frankfurt, and Paris, now occupy the natural middle ground between the US and Asia. Brexit has sharpened this evolution. London is a legacy, declining, niche market. Look at the constituents of the FTSE 100, relative to the S&P 500, or the Europe Stoxx 600. The FTSE 100 has very few what could be called growth stocks. It is a tired, cheap index, which pays a decent yield. It is a reflection of a failure to formulate a comprehensive growth and industrial strategy, which spans many administrations. The FTSE 250 and small cap areas have some smaller, and more interesting constituents. However, they are undervalued relative to global peers, as the UK's relevance in the global financial system is so diminished, that it is barely worth allocating any capital to it. The UK's growth incubator market, AIM, is dead on its feet. Offering a legacy of corporate governance scandals and fraud. It is a tough cycle to break, particularly after Brexit. The Edinburgh Reforms, launched by Chancellor, Jeremy Hunt, a serial failure at cabinet level, have been an embarrassing failure. The damp squid reforms, which amount to little more than regulatory arbitrage, were amusingly referred to a Big Bang 2. Comparing the dismal efforts of the hapless Hunt, to Lawson's reforms in the 1980s, which at the time were very significant, equates to pitching a peashooter against howitzer. Now, after the Spring 2024 Budget, the strategy has the appearance of harassing defined contributions schemes to invest more in UK assets. Markets should stand on their own merits. Also, be cautious about the move to pressure for a greater allocation to private assets. This includes new ventures and private equity. The former, if done meritocratically, and responsibly, is reasonably sensible. The latter is potentially more problematic. Beyond leverage, accounting chicanery, cost cutting, and highly subjective valuations, I have seen little in private equity. As an industry, it is very incestuous, with both the legal and political sectors. As an industry, private equity has done very well out of the process of siphoning off public money, via the privatisation of services which should never the state sector, where the profit motive is immoral. I know of a very deep, and comprehensive study, of this shameful process, which will create quite a scandal, as it leads right into the heart of the financial sector. The FCA's ambitions to be at the forefront of the Cryptocurrency, FinTech and Environmental, Social and Governance (ESG) investment, including sustainability strategies, is simply not viable at the current time. It is quite ridiculous. The WealthTek situation has served as a reminder that the UK is a poorly regulated financial services market, and a key global money laundering centre.

So, what should become of the FCA? Clearly, the regulator needs to be placed into special measures, pending serious reform. The level of incompetence, arrogance, and lack of accountability is extraordinary. The legal impunity, to provide a shield to prevent legal challenges frustrating investigations and prosecutions, has been abused. It has been used to smoother incompetency, and accountability. It has created an arrogant indifference to the suffering of consumers, which I have described as inverted morality. A regulator content to issue false and misleading statements to the public. A regulator which fails to hold itself to the standards expected of those regulated. The UK, in seeking to revive its financial services sector, has addressed the problem from the wrong angle. It has placed the cart before the horse. It is not viable to seek to improve the quality, and competitiveness, both domestically, and internationally, of the financial services sector, without first fixing the regulator. The FCA has a challenging job, which I acknowledge. Some of its intentions are good. Indeed, it enjoys some successes. Somewhat belatedly, challenging banks on deposit and mortgage pricing, and calling out the disgraceful practice of double dipping, being recently examples. The latter takes us back to AJ Bell. Sponsor of The Great North Run. Perhaps they would be better served supporting buy one, get one free deals. Before the FCA raised the issue, their level of profiteering on client deposits was a disgrace. However, there are clear cultural issues. Fixing this requires more than a superficial makeover. People, and institutions, make mistakes. This is inevitable. Both the FCA and HM Treasury need to be humble, and humane, when such incidences occur. It is morally unacceptable to show callous indifference to those most impacted. It creates a poor image for both the financial services sector, and the country. The UK should step back from its absurd ambitions to be a leader in cryptocurrency, fintech, ESG, and sustainability finance. It is too soon. The FCA and HM Treasury have sought to camouflage the catastrophic failings in the WealthTek situation, in pursuit of their unrealistic ambitions. WealthTek clients have paid a price as a result. The use of the time zero approach to conceal the blatant violations of their statutory and operational objectives, with full blessing from HM Treasury. The UK cannot fix the sector, without reforming the regulator.

I will close this chapter out by considering John. John is entitled to defend himself, in a fair legal process. One in full compliance of the European Convention on Human Rights. I have stated throughout the book, that I always hoped that the theories that I developed would be incorrect.

Fundamentally, I wish for those clients impacted in the WealthTek situation to receive back all the money that they have lost. If my theories are correct, I believe that in the early stages of the Sapia relationship, client assets were misused. He is an intelligent man, with a good eye for an opportunity. I came to fear that possible frustrations over a lack of capital to pursue desires and opportunities, were abated by having access to capital. This is a dangerous line to cross, as it is a gross violation of professional duty, and trust. It amounts to a Faustian Pact. A deal with the devil. It may have begun with a personal reconciliation that it would be temporary, and the capital replaced. It surely never ends this way. That voice that evoked the initial temptation, will always returns with greater demands. That adrenaline stimulated by the thought of getting away with it, will not dissipate. Before long, he may have found himself completely embroiled. How do you climb down from such a pedestal of apparent meteoric success? How do you disappoint those who believed in your success? How do you give up the hollow adoration it has created? I found myself wondering if he had created his own metaphysical reality to legitimise it? Surely, this was required when meeting people impacted, some were well acquainted with him. Knowing such actions would devastate their lives. However, thorough the audit, only John will know the complete truth. His actions, and motivations. If there is any truth in the allegations, I would encourage him to look within himself, and find the John who created Vertem Asset Management. The person who wanted to create an innovative, and client centred asset management boutique. Whatever the comforts of wealth, it is not worth it, if it is founded in dishonestly and deception. It is better to live modestly and be honest. I hope he can once again put clients first and help them recuperate as much of their money as possible, in the circumstances. It is not possible to erase the emotional trauma that they have faced. But further damage and anxiety could be avoided. If there has been wrongdoing, as alleged, John is intelligent enough to know that there must be punishment. John is a little older than me. I believe that in time, he is capable of doing good. Any wrongs cannot be erased, but he can finish his life on good terms. His considerable abilities, and intelligence, can, hopefully, be put to positive endeavours. The unpleasant reality is legal professionals are feasting on the misery of WealthTek clients. Like vultures. They have feasted during the special administration process, and are gorging on client assets, as the case progresses through the courts. Nothing has changed from the days of Bleak House. Dickens called it correctly. They feast on misery and misfortune. The sums quoted during the special administration process, and the case, are obscene. The dark side of the UK. I hope John recognises this grave injustice. I miss the early days of Vertem Asset Management. The hope and optimism, that we could do well, by doing well for clients. The days when we put more attention into the portfolios of clients, than our own. I daresay that I was not the easiest person to work with, but it pains me that Vertem Asset Management will now be remembered for a tragedy. A company that started with fine intentions, before being lost to the races. Even Jabez Spencer

Balfour, following an infamously unsuccessful dash to Argentina, accepted his punishment, and went on to reform his life, returning to work until his passing. Although, it was not an easy process. I found myself looking into aspects of his arrest, and trial, along with his incarceration. Some of it was quite disturbing, from the prospective of a legal process. I found my mind turning back to the denial of access for John to his emails and the WealthTek servers. I wondered if he was trying to redeem part of the shortfall. Was there a plan to make good the losses? This is not to excuse the situation. Could it be that the desire to secure a criminal conviction, and cover the embarrassing stream of incompetency, has played a part? If such a motivation does exist, what if it increased the anxiety and losses for WealthTek clients? Could it be that by sticking rigidly to the special administration, and the legal processes, this has benefited professionals, at the expense of clients? This is conjecture, but nonetheless, it must be discounted. There are occasions where history is the best teacher we choose to ignore.

The Great Game of Delusion

This, the last chapter, may well be seen as the most controversial. But, alas, allow me another career digression, before I proceed. Traversing back to my pre-financial services career, I found myself surveying a base metal mine in Uzbekistan. I really liked the Uzbeks, and hope to one day return. My time in the country stimulated my interest in what has come to be termed The Great Game. The intrigue, and interplay, between the British and Russian empires in Central Asia. It wrote people like Alexander Burnes into history. Coming back to point, what it taught me is that there are no such things as good and bad states. Life is not that simple, however binary the media portray it. I have another belief. Bad situations, and failures, do not occur in insolation. The failings of the FCA, and the indifference of HM Treasury, cannot be seen in isolation. They are symptoms of broader failings within the UK. I cannot write an extensive book in the space of a chapter. But I will try to illustrate of areas of difficulty.

As a country, I do not think the UK has come anywhere near acknowledging, and atoning for, the immense damage inflicted on the rest of the world, during its imperial age, and in the period following its decline. The period of empire represented an enormous transfer of wealth, on tragically exploitative terms. Even now, the UK refuses to hand bank hordes of stolen artifacts. The Parthenon Marbles being just one shocking example. Handing back stolen artifacts would be a notable act of contrition. Many of the world's current problems, were forged in the fire of British greed. It is difficult to understand how a process of reconciliation with the difficulties of the past can progress, when the head of state also represents a family which spearheaded the imperial era and were greatly enriched in the process. Look at the land this family benefits from. As with other large land landowners, such as the Duke of Northumberland, and Duke of Westminster, there should be an historic investigation into the origin, and merits, of this grotesque accumulation. A Member of Parliament cannot sit in the House of Commons, without swearing allegiance to the King, despite securing the largest number of votes in their constituency. This takes us to the issues of democracy. The first past the post system that populates the House of Commons, subject to swearing allegiance to a hereditary monarch, cannot be said to be a properly democratic system. It is a managed democracy, structured to protect established political parties, and narrow discourse. It is in many ways a democratic straitjacket, as a large number of votes are wasted. This is compounded by the upper chamber, the House of Lords, which is unelected, and stuffed full of patronage. It is not credible to view such as system beyond that of a carefully managed democracy. As I write this book, the UK had a Prime Minister that was not elected in his role, and was rejected by grassroots party members, while the Foreign Secretary, also unelected, was shoehorned into the House of Lords to occupy the role, unaccountable to the elected chamber. This system is not fit for purpose.

I will turn now to what we frequently hear as the western, liberal, rules-based order. Contrary to media and political narratives, there is no divine document enshrining the superiority of western values. Only western dominated international organisations, which endorse them. Such values, aside from rank hypocrisy, are mere metaphysical constructs, infused with commercial and geopolitical undertones. They could easily be construed as a trojan horse for expanding the influence of the collective west. I am in my late 40s as I write this book. I do not recall a time when the UK was not agitating against a nation, or even group of nations. Sadly, I have lost count of the number of countries that the UK has attacked, without first being subject to hostile action. Perhaps there would be a greater chance for global peace if the collective west gave up its self-proclaimed monopoly on righteousness. Neither does it have engrained superiority. The Robinson Crusoe view of the world is outdated.

Often the reasons for wars are greatly distorted. If we take World War One, the standard theory is that the war started because the Archduke Franz Ferdinand, and his wife, were assassinated in Sarajevo by

Bosnian Serb, Gavrilo Princip. At the basic level this is true. But the roots of a war are more likely to be found in the wars that precede it. In this case, it was the Franco-Prussian war, which began in 1870. The war proved to be a catalyst for German unification. A state that rapidly came to rival Britain industrially, and militarily. If you were to read Winston Churchill's volumes on World War One, the desire to contain Germany, particularly at sea, is very obvious. Britian could not live with a rival state on the continent, which could challenge its naval dominance. It would not accept the right of Germany to establish its own colonies and expand its global trade. It was undoubted containment. Notions of a war against tyranny are very hard to sustain. It was a war of empires. Albeit with different geography, there are so many similarities to the position of the west, led by the US, towards China. The west must dominate the world because western values are superior. The strong echo of history.

While I acknowledge that World War Two became a war against fascism, the prelude was more complicated. Neville Chamberlain, and Lord Halifax, were willing to trade large parts of Europe with Hitler's Germany, for no interference with the British Empire. Hitler departed very little from Mien Kampf. It was only when Hitler advanced beyond the Sudetenland, to invade all of Czechoslovakia, that it was apparent that they had been duped, and no deals could be done. The result being the Polish ultimatum. It is a mistake to interpret this in the context of the UK being a reliable ally of Poland. Such notions were dispensed with after Poland was bartered away to Stalin at Yalta. It many ways this echoed British indifference of the partition of Poland in 1795. Britian's focus was on the acquisition of French overseas territories, amid the chaos of the revolution. Britian has never fought, or sponsored, wars motivated by humanity. It has done so for commerce. I do not mean to suggest that British & Commonwealth service personnel who were engaged in both world wars were not brave. They certainly were. I do, however, question the official narrative given to them for going to war. Governments throughout history have seldom been honest in this respect. I also question whether enough respect has shown to those subjects from the Commonwealth, who often had to fund their own contributions to British wars, in addition to sacrificing their lives.

Bringing matters to more contemporary events, the crisis in Gaza and has its roots in British and French greed and deceptions. Both eyed the spoils of the Ottoman Empire, which dissolved after World War One. The consequences have been tragic ever since. Before progressing, I must be clear that I am no antisemitic. I am not even sure that is the correct term to use, as unless I am mistaken, the Semitic people were not unilaterally tied to a religion. Either way, I believe in religious toleration, finding myself influenced by Voltaire's Treatise on Tolerance. However, I find myself greatly distressed by the plight of the Palestinian people. I do not condone the actions of Hamas. I also recognise Israel's right to self-defence and understand their anger. But these matters aside, what I have witnessed in Gaza has all the appearance of genocide. The lack of meaningful protest from senior UK politicians has been disgraceful. They have in many ways been complicit in the genocide, running down the clock as the death tolls soars. It is a dark blotch on the conscious of the UK. Instead, a culture of fear pervades the country, for any person expressing concern for the welfare of the Palestinian people. Anyone doing so is labelled a terrorist sympathiser, and an antisemite. Nothing I write in this book should be considered in this way. I do not want to see Jewish people harmed. I want to see them live in peace and dignity, as I do the Palestinians. Self-defence cannot be allowed to become genocide. The ineptness and cowardice of UK politicians should not be used as justification to harass Jewish people. This is not the way forward either. I hope Israel can elect a Prime Minister who can lead the country to peace, not perpetual war. However, Muslims must wonder where to cast their votes. All the major parties must appear unfriendly. The UK has attacked Muslim countries, without first being attacked, and the recent acts offering the appearance of genocide in Gaza, have evokes only tokenistic expressions of concern. This is in addition to the fear of speaking out, and being labelled antisemitic and, or a terrorist sympathiser. Instead of sneering at the government of South Africa for seeking to end the genocide, the UK should have been proud to support them. The citizens of South Africa, should, in this instance, be proud of their government.

I want to also take a brief look at matters in Ukraine. Of course, the easiest way of looking at the situation is to take a binary stance, that the west is all good, and the Russian Federation, all bad. Now, before I am criticised, I do not condone war and invasion, because innocent people suffer the most. Neither do I condone acts of terrorism, for the same reasons. But I also recognise that nothing is as simple as good and bad. If we are candid with ourselves, since independence in 1991, both the west, and Russia, have competed for interests in Ukraine. In addition, since independence, Ukraine has offered an appearance of a nation torn. A nation pulled both ways, east and west. The success of nations such as Poland, and the Czech Republic, particularly the historically intricate relationship with the former, was an obvious pull west. The pull to the European Union. Equally, in the east of the country, we cannot deny the strong cultural links to Russia. It may be argued that Russian concerns about NATO encirclement, and the mistreatment of ethnic Russians in Ukraine, have been exaggerated, but they certainly cannot be dismissed without foundation. It could be argued that the war has engendered a tragedy for both sides. It was clear from the start of the war that to drive Russian troops back to the other side of the border, would require NATO troops, for which there was no appetite. The Ukrainians have fought very bravely, but they do not have the manpower required to push Russian troops out of entrenched positions. In addition, the idea that sanctions would break the Russian Federation, was never straightforward. The Russian Federation can heat and feed itself. By way of comparison, the UK can do neither. If the UK faced the same sanctions as those levied on the Russian Federation, it would collapse within weeks. Therefore, a stalemate ensued. The west, and very pertinently the UK, are obsessed with Putin. The relentless coverage of the 2024 Presidential Election being a case in point. In some respects, it is very odd, as it no doubt strengthens his position. Whatever, the UK, thinks of Putin, ultimately, he is a matter for the people of the Russian Federation. This will be countered by those who claim he is a tyrant. History has taught us that the Russian people are quite capable of disposing of leaders, be they monarchs, or politicians, when they have stepped beyond their station. In addition, it is morally problematic for the UK to cry outrage at an invasion, when it has a long history of aggressive action towards other countries. Putting Putin aside, history reveals that Britain has been far more aggressive towards Russia, than the reverse. I am merely illustrating that the west is best model does not stand up well to scrutiny. One side is not all good, and one side is not all bad. The dynamics of the Crimean War are interesting. As the Ottoman Empire fell into decline, the Russian Empire saw opportunities to push into the Balkans, supporting what they considered to be oppressed Christians in the process. This alarmed the British and French, who felt the risk of the Russian Empire potentially reclaiming Constantinople for the Orthodox faith and controlling the Black Sea. The aggression was initiated by the British and French. Moving forward in history, I want to share a quote taken from the book, Ace of Spies, The True Story of SIDNEY REILLY, by Andrew Cook. Some readers will note a link between my interest in the man known in the UK as Sidney Reilly, and Port Arthur, covered above. The quote below is part of a note sent from Archibald Sinclair to Winston Churchill.

Secretary of State

I hope you will find time to read these two short memoranda by my remarkable MI1c friend Reilly They contain a concrete proposal for the bringing about the Downfall of the Soviet government by economic means and for putting us in a position at the earliest possible moment to obtain food and raw materials from Soviet Russia.

Now, of course, one might have taken a dislike to the Soviet government of the 1920s. But look at the ultimate motivation. Again, leaving Putin aside, if I were a current citizen of the Russian Federation, I am not confident that I would see the current motivations of the UK, as hugely different from those outlined in the above quote. There is another historical inconvenience. If we were to study three great wars involving Britain, those being The Napoleonic Wars, along with World Wars One and Two, had there not have been the enormous sacrifice of Russian lives, each could well have ended very differently. Swinging back to the war in Ukraine, the west, and certainly the UK, need to be very careful to delineate between concerns for the Ukrainian people, and the desire to achieve regime change in the Russian Federation. We also need honesty over interference. There is great outcry of Russian interference in the UK, some with obvious justification. But can we be naïve enough to believe that the UK, and its allies, do not conduct nefarious activities in the Russian Federations? There is a sad reality to the current divisions. For this, readers will need to look at a map. Look at the Eurasian landmass. Think of the obvious synergies that exist between Europe and Asia, including China, India, and the Russian Federation, amongst others. It is a great shame that all this potential cannot be harnessed, on mutually respectful terms, without one side claiming superior values over the other. What a lost opportunity this is. There would be a vast dynamic of people, food, and valuable resources. But this would change the balance of power within the global economy. The economic weight of the world would tilt from the from the west to the east. Most notably, the US hegemony would be diluted. There was a glimpse of this prior to the war in Ukraine. This was seen in the very successful trading relationship between China, Germany, and The Russian Federation. Since the war, each economy has suffered. Soon we will hear scare stories of Russian, and likely Chinese interference in UK & US elections. Take a listen to the Panaroma episode, Trump: The Sequel. The episode is fronted by state sponsored mouthpieces, Justin Webb, and Marianna Spring. I do not support Trump, nor do I Biden, but this output can only be seen as election interference with a bias against the former. Be careful of Spring. She plays an interesting game. The champion of busting misinformation could easily be considered as an agent to sponsor its proliferation. It is high time we are relieved from the threat of force to pay the wages of provocateurs such as Spring. On the topic of censorship, it is noticeable that debates on the scale of corruption in Ukraine, are very active in the US. The topic has been censored in the UK. In the context of his past career, it will be interesting to see how imagine of Zelenskyy stands amid the scrutiny of time.

Let us stay return to China. When I suffer myself to look at the censorious, and often racially fused British media, alongside fairly prolific Russia and Islamophobia, there is Sinophobia. It is possible that people can take an issue with the Chinese Communist Party, and their mode of government. But a choice must be made. It is not viable, or even acceptable, to take the stance that we will take the benefits of trade but dictate to the Chinese over how their society should be run. If you trade with China, or other countries, this does not come with the right to provide a lecture on governance. You either accept the differences on mutually respectful terms, or refrain from trade. You cannot have it both ways. Stepping back to the Thatcher era, a rather naïve decision was made to deindustrialise the UK, and orientate the economy towards services, and in, particularly consumption. China has fulfilled the desire of UK population to consume competitively priced products. Furthermore, a good many academic institutions have done very well from Chinese money. Once again, history shows the UK to have been the legacy aggressor, with the opium wars being a prominent example. While often derided in the UK, the Century of Shame is a very important motivation for the Chinese drive to never again to be at the mercy of foreign powers. As with the Russian Federation, the idea that the Chinese can be won over with western values, is nonsense. The UK, and the collective west, should perhaps be careful what they wish for. Any ideas that the vast and diverse populations of China, and the Russian Federation, would fall neatly into westerns style managed democracies, is complete folly. As with the Russians, the Chinese have shown themselves capable of disposing of leaders, when they have lost the respect of the people. The world will be a far more stable, and peaceful, if notion of western superiority is replaced with a consensus to be respectful of differences.

Throughout my life, and no doubt for a long period before, the UK has struggled to come to terms with its relative decline. This has made it a very quarrelsome and aggressive state. Just as it is hard to pinpoint the start of the rise of the British Empire, so it is to identify the beginning of its decline. I often look to the Boar War, which was eventually won after Kitchener pioneered modern war crimes. This is what it took to overcome the battle-hardened Boars. The world took note, particularly, the unified Germans. The British army suddenly appeared far from invincible. The world wars that followed, accelerated the decline. The savvy, and opportunistic, Americans realised that they could replace the exhausted British, and become the new hegemon, without the incumbency of an empire. As its empire melted away, the UK, to a large extent, turned away from the Commonwealth, towards Europe. Up until leaving the European Union, the UK was a difficult and troublesome member, with England unable to let go of its imperial instructs. This was only partially mitigated in foreign policy terms, by occupying the role of the embittered bagman of the US. Much of this was observed in the referendum, with leave arguments little more than echoes of imperialism. Ideas of a liberated nation that could return to its free trading heritage. This was fantasy. The British Empire was more about coercive trade, enforced by a very powerful navy. Some arguments touched on boosting London as a financial centre. As noted above, the sun has been setting on London for some time. The integrated European markets are far more attractive for major businesses to list. London will likely only attract businesses with greater obscurity, and more challenging corporate governance. The WealthTek situation has shown that the UK has retained its reputation as a key money laundering centre. The calamitous failures of the FCA, has taken the regulation of the market to levels below what is expected of a frontier market. Exciting new trade deals have been elusive. You can see how the balance of power has changed. Negotiations with India have been interesting to observe. India holds the sway now. A very humbling experience for the former colonial master. Brexit has posed great questions as to the viability of the UK, in its current form. Scotland is naturally more orientated towards Europe, given its history of seeking protection against English dominance. Scotland should look to Ireland for inspiration. Look through the economic scare stories and continue to press for independence. The EU should make it clear that the there is a place for Scotland. The country needs its identity and must remember that no court can thwart the will of the people. Unfortunately, in the near term, the complacency of the Scottish Nationalist Party, has provided the Westminster parties with the opportunity to undermine the independence movement. I hope the people regain their sense of orientation. Similarly, Northern Ireland can take the opportunity to draw inspiration from the Republic. The challenge is overcoming some intra-religious disputes, but, surely, this can be achieved for a better, and more prosperous future. Unfettered access to the EU. Demographic trends will likely prove to be irresistible. It would be more problematic for the UK, in its current form, to rejoin the EU, due to the embedded imperialism, and assumed air of superiority of England. Since the departure of the UK from the EU, it has been noticeable that the block, with a few exceptions, is a more harmonious place. It is much more manageable without England.

It is somewhat ironic that since leaving the EU, the UK remained vexed by immigration. But there is a difference. Those who seek to come now, are from far less developed locations. If you think back to the 2016 EU referendum, it was the Poles who were spoken of as taking jobs and driving down wages and so on. Now, the Poles are unlikely to arrive, as the UK is no longer an attractive destination. I have watched both countries for nearly twenty years. It is a story of relative progress and decline. When I first visited Poland, the infrastructure was crumbling, and the economy was relatively underdeveloped. Now, it is the UK which suffers crumbling infrastructure. If you visit the major Polish cities, you will note that they are already at UK levels, and in some cases are more superior. I do wonder if we will see educated British citizens emigrate in greater numbers, rather than receiving the equivalents from newly joined EU states. Immigration, while still a highly topical issue, is often misunderstood. Much of the modern immigration is driven by global inequality, which is exacerbated by climate change. If I am correct, emigration from the UK will see relatively well-educated people leave in greater numbers, owing to declining standards of living. Adding to incentives to leave, are high taxes, grossly overvalued property, corruption and excessive welfarism. My advice to well-educated younger workers is, look abroad for a better life.

Closely related to the issue of immigration, is an unpleasant racist undertone, most notably in England. We see it in all walks of life, politics, sport and in the media. You could argue that Scotland, and Northern Ireland, paid a heavy price in 2016, for what was in essence, a fit of racism in England. I do not need to look far for institutionalised racism. Both South Tyneside Council, and Northumbria Police, are staunchly institutionally racist. The Cabinet of South Tyneside Council embody, and promote, racism and corruption. I was reviewing some of the material, and it will somewhat sadly bring horrendous shame to the region. In one clip, a manager at the council, laughed, shrugged, and said "This is the North East" when asked why all her staff are white? There is a large line of corruption which runs right through the local authority, legal profession, and into the financial services industry. Hundreds of hours of footage have been collated. It is a typical Labour council. They do not want people to be independent. Dependency is their business. This is what creates the opportunities for local councillors to skim off public money. When citizens take responsibility for their affairs, these opportunities do not exist. Corruption is a significant problem in the UK. You do not have to look far to find it. It is every bit as bad as that which attracts criticism from the UK, in reference to other states. The UK is very vulnerable in this regard. The country has often relied on censorship, and legal tyranny, to cover domestic corruption, but this is becoming unsustainable. There are very willing, and fertile, markets for such material.

The country is crippled by self-serving institutions and welfarism. In blunt terms, largescale misuse of public money, and worklessness. It is a very challenging combination. It has led to a record of low growth, and poor productivity. You cannot even get the police to do anything. Think about grocery inflation. I encourage readers to think about how this has been exacerbated by the police refusing to help apprehend rampant shopkeepers. When you visit your local supermarket, take a look at the extra investment made to prevent shoplifters. All this is passed on to consumers. Business rates, and the taxes paid by consumers, have paid the police twice to deal with the issue. They are not interested. The lure of the takeaway menu, and catching motorists travelling marginally above the speed limit, have proven too great. In the north east of England, we have a Police and Crime Commissioner. A thoroughly useless role. Millions of pounds wasted. The longstanding incumbent wrote to residents of South Tyneside pledging to clamp down on illegal motorbikes, years before the Covid-19 pandemic. The perpetrators simply do not take the police seriously. Just as the FCA has abandoned WealthTek clients, so our public officials, including politicians, have abandoned the people who fund them. The role of Police and Crime Commissioner is grifting in all but name. The people of the region do not even know what they are funding. An economy will never achieve a sustainable level of attractive growth, if too much money is siphoned off for unproductive, wasteful, spending. It is somewhat ironic that politicians complain about popularism, and the legacy media fret about alternatives. Both reflect a wholesale lack of trust from the public. The current crop of politicians are the worst in my lifetime. The Prime Minister is not even wanted by his party members. Keir Starmer looks little more than a frontman for the legal industry. In the event of a Labour victory, expect a whole host new initiatives to siphon public money into private equity owned business, and to his chums in the legal sector. We can only hope that his appetite for warmongering is not comparable to the last legal frontman put up by Labour. We saw the real Starmer when his privileged pension deal was revealed by the media. The leader of the Liberal Democrats shamelessly abandoned persecuted victims of the Post Office scandal. Instead of seeing themselves as the problem, our politicians conjure new methods of censorship, to evade due accountability. The biggest threat to the managed democracy in the UK, are those who represent it. Each of three has been shamelessly quiet on genocide in Gaza. They are complicit. They are morally unfit for office. For large parts of the population, there is also a lack of spiritual leadership, which rests with the failure of the Christianity, and, most strikingly, the Church of England, to remain relevant. It is morally difficult for the Church of England, as it was born out of the grand theft, and tyranny, of Henry VIII. Occasionally, I run past a church in Hebburn, which now hosts a Buddhist Meditation Centre. What we are seeing is minority religions filling the spiritual void. They have maintained, and, in some cases, are growing their relevance. They still value the family as a bedrock unit of society. Justin Welby and his predecessors have been a disaster. Large elements of UK society worship chavocrats, known as social media influencers. Social media is somewhat of an enigma. A decentralised media source, which is a trojan horse for censorship. The more people use it, the less free they become. As odd as it may seem, freedom of thought, and speech, will be more accessible by the more classic modes of in-person interactions, meeting and talking.

The UK risks becoming a failing state. It must cease picking fights overseas, as a way of masking very challenging domestic problems. The country simply does not have the moral authority to play the virtuous global citizen. There are positives. If you venture into the private sector, there many good companies. But they are undermined by poor political leadership, and self-serving institutions. As I neared the end of writing the book, the FCA set out its plan for the year ahead in an update, published on 19th March 2024. Chief Executive, Nikhil Rathi, wrote about working towards becoming a world-class data-led regulator. This is an awful long way from the role of the Potemkin Village idiot, who ignores whistleblowers, and has no means to track a bankruptcy. It is absolute fantasy.

I return to my earlier comment about there being no such thing as good and bad states. It is very easy for us to lapse into the Robinson Crusoe view and cast the UK in the role as the civilising force in a dangerous world. As inconvenient as it maybe, the UK is as, and in in many cases more, belligerent and corrupt as those countries considered to be foes. It many respects it is the same issue encountered with the FCA. Both country, and regulator, need to fix their considerable internal problems before projecting themselves onto the wider world. I contend that HM Treasury recognising the human costs of the failures of its errant subordinate, would represent a positive step in this direction. Countries purporting to be good, do not allow the most innocent to suffer the greatest, in the interests of preserving the reputations of those who failed them.